AF575648

Library of Congress Control Number: 2022944505

Designed by Justin Watkinson
Type set in Impact/Minion Pro/Univers LT Std

ISBN: 978-0-7643-6645-1
Printed in India

Published by Schiffer Publishing, Ltd.
4880 Lower Valley Road
Atglen, PA 19310
Phone: (610) 593-1777; Fax: (610) 593-2002
Email: Info@schifferbooks.com
Web: www.schifferbooks.com

For our complete selection of fine books on this and related subjects, please visit our website at www.schifferbooks.com. You may also write for a free catalog.

Schiffer Publishing's titles are available at special discounts for bulk purchases for sales promotions or premiums. Special editions, including personalized covers, corporate imprints, and excerpts, can be created in large quantities for special needs. For more information, contact the publisher.

We are always looking for people to write books on new and related subjects. If you have an idea for a book, please contact us at proposals@schifferbooks.com.

Acknowledgments

This book would not have been possible without the generous assistance and resources of many friends and institutions, among them Tom Kailbourn, Tracy White, Stan Piet, Scott Taylor, Dana Bell, Robert Bohlmann, the National Museum of Naval Aviation, the National Museum of the United States Air Force, the San Diego Air and Space Museum, the American Aviation Historical Society, the Naval History and Heritage Command, and the National Archives. Many of the photos in this book were scanned by my wife, Denise, without whose help and support this book would not have been possible.

Contents

Introduction

The Consolidated PBY is the most readily recognized—and widely produced—flying-boat design ever made. The specifications and design of the PBY drew on lessons learned by the US Navy through a series of prior flying boats that stretched back to a proposal by RAdm. David Taylor in 1917 that a flying boat capable of crossing the Atlantic be developed. Taylor's proposal was to manifest itself in the Curtiss NC-1 of 1918. During the interwar years, the US Navy utilized a number of types of flying boats (an aircraft in which the fuselage also serves a boat hull) and float planes (an aircraft capable of operating from water, but whose fuselage is supported by floats or pontoons).

By the mid-1920s, Consolidated Aircraft, located in Buffalo, New York, had become a notable supplier of flying boats to the US Navy. Under the guidance of pioneering aviation industrialist Reuben Hollis Fleet, the firm had developed the Navy's first monoplane flying boat, the Model 9 Admiral. This aircraft was designed by Consolidated's Isaac Macklin Laddon in response to a Navy requirement for an all-metal patrol aircraft capable of flying directly to Panama, Alaska, or Hawaii from stateside bases.

While Consolidated also built the prototype of that aircraft, which the Navy designated XPY-1, they did not secure the production contract. That contract was awarded to the Glenn L. Martin Company, which underbid Consolidated and produced duplicates under the designation P3M. Although Martin produced the aircraft for the Navy, Consolidated built and sold variations of the XPY-1 design to the commercial market, building and selling fourteen aircraft that were marketed as the Commodore.

The Consolidated Model 22 Ranger, a 1931 design, was the next flying boat bought by the Navy in quantity, with forty-seven examples in three variations being delivered to the service.

Thus, it was not surprising that when the Navy was seeking an improved flying boat the next year, Consolidated was one of the firms asked to submit a design. In response to this request, in 1932 Consolidated offered a new design, which they referred to as their Model 28. The Navy was sufficiently impressed with the design advanced by Consolidated that on October 28, 1933, a contract was issued for a single prototype with the Navy designation XP3Y-1. Douglas had offered a competing design and was also awarded a contract for a prototype of their aircraft, the XP3D-1. The XP3Y-1 was built at Consolidated's Buffalo plant. It was partially disassembled and shipped by train to the Navy installation at Anacostia, Maryland, outside Washington, DC. The XP3Y-1 first flew on March 21, 1935, with company pilot William Wheatley at the controls. The Navy was pleased to determine that the performance of the aircraft exceeded the requirements. Although it was determined that the design did need some further improvement, early tests showed that the aircraft had the potential to be a patrol bomber, and thus in October 1935 the aircraft was returned to Consolidated to be so modified.

In February 1928, the US Navy granted Consolidated Aircraft a contract to produce a prototype of the Navy's first monoplane flying boat. It featured two vertical tails, an open cockpit, and two Pratt & Whitney engines. The XPY-1 first took to the air on January 10, 1929. *San Diego Air and Space Museum*

The next step in Consolidated Aircraft's development of flying boats, the XP2Y-1 prototype, was an improvement of the XPY-1. Contracted for on May 26, 1931, the aircraft was initially powered by a trio of 575-horsepower Wright Cyclone engines and featured a short wing beneath the main airfoil. *San Diego Air and Space Museum*

Shortly after the XP2Y-1's first flight on March 26, 1932, and the start of its test program, it was determined that the top-mounted engine offered no real benefit, and it was eliminated. The XP2Y-1 also differed from the XPY-1 by having an enclosed cockpit.

In July 1931, the Navy granted Consolidated a contract for twenty-three P2Y-1s. The last of those aircraft was converted to the XP2Y-2, with engines enclosed in nacelles faired into the leading edge of the wing, rather than underslung as on the P2Y-1.

The new engine installation and a few other improvements brought about a 10 mph increase in the aircraft's top speed and an increase in range. Suitably impressed, the Navy ordered twenty-three of the new model, which was designated the P2Y-3. *San Diego Air and Space Museum*

So pleased was the Navy with the improved performance of the P2Y-3 that a conversion program was undertaken on the P2Y-1. Dubbed the Ranger, all the P2Y-1 aircraft received the new engine installation and were redesignated P2Y-2. *San Diego Air and Space Museum*

CHAPTER 1

The Flying Boats

The XP3Y-1 and XP3D-1 were remarkably similar in performance, and the firms had similar capabilities, leaving the Navy to decide which aircraft would enter production largely on price. Douglas bid approximately $110,000 per aircraft, while Consolidated, having previously been burned on the XPY-1, bid a more modest $90,000 per aircraft and thus, on June 29, 1935, was awarded a production contract for sixty aircraft. In October 1935, the Navy received some desired publicity when the XP3Y-1, which now sported a redesigned rudder, was flown by Lt. Cmdr. Knefler McCinnis from Norfolk, Virginia, to Coco Solo, Panama Canal Zone, and then on to San Francisco, arriving on October 15 and setting a new world distance record for a seaplane.

Five days later, the aircraft flew to San Diego for the dedication of the new Consolidated facility there, which would replace the former Buffalo, New York, plant. While in San Diego, the XP3Y-1 was modified with a rotating nose gun position, further improved tail, and, notably, improved 850-horsepower Pratt & Whitney R-1830-64 Twin Wasp engines. The new engines raised the top speed of the aircraft at 8,000 feet from 169 to 184 mph.

Reflecting the flying boat's new role as a patrol bomber, the Navy redesignated the aircraft XPBY-1. The first production PBY-1 was delivered in September 1936, and on October 5 of that year VP-11 became the first patrol squadron to receive one.

Even before the first PBY-1 was delivered, on July 25, 1936, the Navy ordered fifty improved PBY-2 aircraft, the first of which were accepted by the Navy in May 1937. The last PBY-1 was delivered the next month.

This order was followed by sixty-six PBY-3s on November 27, 1936, and a thirty-three-aircraft order for PBY-4 flying boats was placed on December 18, 1937. The first PBY-3 was accepted in November 1937, a year after it was ordered, with the remaining PBY-3s on the order being delivered between March and August 1938. The first of the PBY-4s was accepted in May 1938, with a further thirty-one being delivered between October 1938 and June 1939. The remaining aircraft was delayed for modification.

In December 1939, the US Navy ordered two hundred PBY-5s, the first large order for the aircraft placed by the American military after World War I. The first of these was accepted in September 1940. The PBY-5 featured many improvements over the previous models, including improved 1,200-horsepower R-1830-82 engines and the .50-caliber waist gun blisters, which would become characteristic of the PBY.

Orders from Britain (which had previously trialed a PBY-4), France, and Canada, totaling 174 similar Model 28-5Ms, were also received by Consolidated. After France capitulated to Germany in 1940, their aircraft were instead delivered to Great Britain, where they were bestowed the name "Catalina." The US Navy adopted that name for the PBY in October 1941.

The XP3Y-1 grew out of a 1932 US Navy requirement for a new patrol flying boat with a gross weight of 25,000 pounds and a range of 3,000 miles at a 100 mph cruising speed. The following year, the Navy issued Consolidated a contract to produce one prototype aircraft based on the company's design. The result was the XP3Y-1, which made its first flight on March 28, 1935. As can be seen in this photo of the plane during tests at Naval Air Station (NAS) Anacostia on April 23, 1935, the plane had the hallmarks of what would become the PBY Catalina, including the parasol wing mounted on a pylon, retractable floats, low cockpit canopy, and provisions for a bow turret. *American Aviation Historical Society*

Two handlers dressed in wetsuits stand in the water next to the XP3Y-1 at Anacostia while another handler leans over the port strut. Consolidated Aircraft designated the XP3Y-1 as Model 28, while the US Navy assigned it Bureau Number (BuNo) 9459. *National Museum of Naval Aviation*

The XP3Y-1 was photographed on April 10, 1935, several weeks after its initial flight. The floats were mounted on retracting struts; when raised, the floats formed the actual wingtips. Unlike the XPY-1 and P2Y, the XP3Y-1 had a single vertical fin and rudder. *San Diego Air and Space Museum*

The XP3Y-1's rudder underwent several revisions. Here is the first design, with a trailing edge that was straight and vertical. As was the case with the P2Ys, the engines of the XP3Y-1 were mounted in nacelles protruding from the leading edge of the wing. *San Diego Air and Space Museum*

The XP3Y-1 rests on the water at NAS Anacostia, District of Columbia, on April 23, 1935, during trials. During trials several months later, problems were encountered with the directional stability of the rudder, and Consolidated took measures to correct them. *San Diego Air and Space Museum*

Consolidated's fix for the XP3Y-1's rudder problems was to install a redesigned rudder on the tail. It had a straight trailing edge like that of the first rudder, but the trailing edge was set at an angle, as seen in this photo of the plane lying in the water near an Omaha-class light cruiser. *San Diego Air and Space Museum*

Crewmen manhandle the XP3Y-1 while naval officers observe the proceedings. The second design of the rudder is present. Aft of the wing on each side of the hull was a sliding panel with a small window, and a man is standing up in the open hatch. *San Diego Air and Space Museum*

Commanded by K. McGinnis, the crew of the XP3Y-1 pose for a photo at the time the aircraft set a new nonstop flight record of 3,443 miles, from Panama to NAS Alameda, in October 1935. The floats are retracted, showing how they form the wingtips when raised. *National Museum of Naval Aviation*

The XP3Y-1 takes off during mid-1936. After the second version of the rudder exhibited problems, a third version, seen here, was installed. This rudder's trailing edge had a curved shape. Black bituminous asphalt paint is on the bottom of the hull and floats. *San Diego Air and Space Museum*

During Consolidated's final tests of the plane, the XP3Y-1 flies over San Diego Bay on May 16, 1936, with North Island at the center of the photo and the harbor at the bottom. Less than a week later, the company would transfer the aircraft to the Navy. *National Museum of Naval Aviation*

The XP3Y-1 displays its port side during a flight over the hills near San Diego, California, on May 16, 1936. Once this prototype had demonstrated the capability of carrying bombs, it was redesignated XPBY-1, the "B" standing for bomber. *San Diego Air and Space Museum*

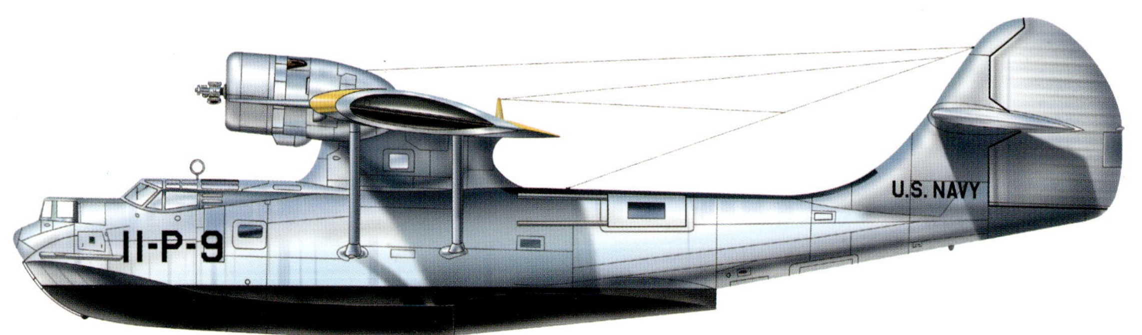

In 1937, this PBY-1 of VP-11 had a paint scheme of Aluminum above the waterline, black below the waterline, and Chrome Yellow on the wing top. Control surfaces were doped fabric. The "11-P-9" code on the side of the hull referred to the ninth aircraft of VP-11.

Following successful initial tests of the XP3Y-1/XPBY-1 prototype in the spring of 1935, the US Navy contracted with Consolidated Aircraft in June 1935 for sixty PBY-1s. Virtually identical to the prototype, the PBY-1 was delivered to the Navy beginning in September 1936. Powering this flying boat were two Pratt & Whitney R-1830-64 engines. Shown here is a PBY-1 of Utility Squadron 4 (VJ-4), marked with the so-called Neutrality Patrol national insignia between the cockpit and the bow turret, as specified in a March 19, 1940, directive by the Bureau of Aeronautics. Visible atop the hull (as the fuselage was called) aft of the wing is a tow-target reel. *American Aviation Historical Society*

The first PBY-1, BuNo 0102, sits on a ramp on October 22, 1936. It bears markings for VP-6 and is fitted with beaching gear, consisting of detachable landing gear attached to the sides of the hull below the wing and on the underside of the rear of the hull. *National Museum of Naval Aviation*

Seen from the front on October 22, 1936, PBY-1 number 1, assigned to VP-6, demonstrates just how little clearance there was between the two propellers. Also evident is the extent to which the bow turret diminished the pilot's and copilot's field of view forward. *National Archives*

As evident in this view of the PBY-1 from the starboard side, the X-shaped brace for the float assembly is actually composed of two V-shaped braces joined together. These braces also serve as the retraction link for the float. *National Archives*

In a view from the aft starboard quarter of the first PBY-1, further details of the arrangement of the floats and their braces are visible. Faintly visible at the top center of the wing is the numeral "6," representing VP-6, redesignated VP-23 in 1939. *National Archives*

A view of the first PBY-1 from directly aft emphasizes the squat shape of the hull and the positioning of the horizontal stabilizers. In addition to the pylon, which was the main support for the wing, there were two diagonal braces on each side. *National Archives*

The inboard end of the port elevator of the first PBY-1 is displayed; it was angled to give clearance to the movement of the rudder. The elevators would be redesigned for the PBY-2. Also in view is the tail beaching gear and the BuNo on the vertical fin. *National Archives*

A closer view is offered of the tail beaching gear on a PBY-1. Two 5.00 × 4 aluminum-alloy wheels with 5.00 × 4 six-ply, smooth-contour rubber tires are on a shock-mounted swiveling knuckle at the bottom of a V-strut, which is secured to attachment points on the bottom of the hull. The V-strut is strengthened with a single strut attached to the swiveling knuckle, and secured with a pin to the towing lug at the upper right of the photo. Attached to the swivel knuckle is a socket into which is inserted the steering bar. *National Archives*

The PBY-1 had an anchor, stowed in the small compartment with the door open. One end of the anchor line is secured to the anchor, and the other end leads to the anchor cable reel inside the anchor box. A line called the pendant, which was used to take up the weight of the anchor, is secured on one end to the anchor cable and on the other end to the fitting visible on the bottom of the hull. Another line, called the lizard, is secured on one end to the pendant and on the other to the mooring post by the turret. *National Archives*

The port main beaching gear of a PBY-1 is displayed close-up in a October 3, 1936, Consolidated factory photo. It consisted of a rigid strut with two Hayes 11.00 × 12 wheels with 11.00 × 12 eight-ply, smooth-contour Goodrich low-pressure tires on a swiveling knuckle. The top of the strut was secured to the upper fitting, recessed in the bottom of the fairing of the forward wing strut. Two brackets on the strut held two long pins, which secured the bottom bracket to the lower fitting, riveted to the chine of the hull. *National Archives*

The anchor is folded up for storage in its compartment on the port side of the bow. Placards with instructions on handling the anchor and its lines are affixed to the inside of the door. The manila rope visible inside the compartment is the lizard. At the top of the door is a snap fitting for holding the door open. Just aft of the anchor box is a retractable step. To the right is an on/off switch for the anchor lights. To the upper left, a part of one of the clear panels of the bow turret is in view. *National Archives*

A Consolidated Aircraft factory photo taken on July 15, 1936, illustrates the aluminum-alloy plating on the forward part of the hull of a partially completed PBY-1. A good view is available of the turret ring, bombardier's window, and anchor box hatch. *National Archives*

An October 1936 Consolidated Aircraft photo shows the bow turret, armed with a Browning .30-caliber machine gun. Although the turret had Plexiglas windows, there was a large open area on the roof of the turret. Also shown is the door of the anchor box. *National Archives*

In a 1936 view inside the bombardier's compartment in the bow of a PBY-1, the .30-caliber machine gun for the turret is stowed in brackets on the starboard side of the compartment. The bombardier doubled as turret gunner in the PBYs. To the left are the bombardier's seat, kneeling cushion, and bombardier's window, and, at the upper left, the turret. The round panel to the right of the bombardier's window was removable and allowed the bombardier to clean the bomb-aiming window in flight if necessary. *National Archives*

The port wingtip float is shown in the extended position in a Consolidated Aircraft photo from October 1936. These floats were of all-metal construction, with aluminum-alloy stressed skin, and they gave the PBY-1 lateral stability while on the water. A recess on the underside of the wing accommodated the drag panel (the major support structure for the float) and the V-struts when the float was raised. A slot in that recess provided room for movement of the screw jack, which actuated the raising and lowering of the float. *National Archives*

The port float is raised, showing how the float formed the wingtip. Also apparent is the manner in which the drag panel of the float assembly fits in the recess in the wing. Next to the float on the leading edge of the wing is the red-colored port navigation light. *National Archives*

Because of the height of the engines of the Catalina, Consolidated Aircraft developed an A-frame boom that attached to the engine and was braced by stays and fitted with a hoist, to lift or lower the propeller when it was necessary to perform maintenance. *National Archives*

The starboard engine installation of a PBY-1 is viewed from the wing, facing forward. In the foreground, with the black box on top, is the top of the starboard oil tank, with a capacity of 47 US gallons. Jutting up from the tank is the oil filler tube and cap. On either side of the oil filler tube is an engine exhaust outlet. In the background, some of the hinged panels of the engine cowl are open. *National Archives*

The cockpit of a PBY-1 is viewed from bulkhead number 2 at the rear of the compartment, facing forward. The pilot's seat is to the left and the copilot's seat is to the right. The control wheels are on a control yoke that extends across the cockpit. *National Archives*

From the center of the cockpit, facing upward and aft, between the seats on bulkhead 2 are the pilot's communications controls and electrical panel. On the roof are windows that double as escape hatch doors, and the pilot's throttle and fuel mixture controls. *National Archives*

This view of the bombardier's compartment of a PBY-1 was taken from the cockpit through an open door in a canvas screen, meant to keep drafts out of the cockpit. To the right are racks for .30-caliber ammunition boxes; stowed to the left is the turret cover. *National Archives*

Tests of the XP3Y-1 had proven the flying boat's aptitude as a bomber, and provisions for mounting bombs were designed into the PBY-1. Six 100-pound bombs are shackled to two bomb racks under the wing of a PBY-1 in a September 24, 1936, photo. *National Archives*

Larger bombs could also be carried on the PBY-1, such as this inert 500-pound bomb being hoisted to a bomb rack with a streamlined fairing. On the near side of the bomb is a portable work platform, secured to fasteners on the bottom of the wing. *National Archives*

A torpedo could also be carried under each wing, as indicated in this September 1937 photo of a Mk. 13 torpedo secured to a rack under the wing of a PBY-1. More details are visible of the portable platforms, which greatly facilitated the work of the crews. *National Archives*

A 1,000-pound bomb is being hoisted to the rack under the port side of the wing of a PBY-1. PBYs could carry the Mk. 5, Mk. 9, or Mk. 13 1,000-pound bomb, each with the Mk. 21 nose fuse and Mk. 23 tail fuse. In addition, PBYs could carry the Mk. 7 water-filled practice bomb. A protective cover of what appears to be kraft paper has been applied to the upper part of the hull of the flying boat. Some of the support frame for the engine is at the upper left. *National Archives*

The radio/navigation compartment of a PBY-1, directly aft of the cockpit, is viewed facing forward. To the left are the navigator's table and seat. On the right side of the compartment are the radioman's seat and radio-transmitting equipment. *National Archives*

The waist compartment of a PBY-1 is viewed facing forward, with bulkhead number 6, a watertight bulkhead, in the background. A machine gun is stowed on each side of the hull, and two extra machine guns are secured on each side of the catwalk. *National Archives*

The port waist hatch (*top*) and the .30-caliber machine gun and mount for that position are viewed. The gun is mounted in a swiveling stirrup, allowing the gun to be swung down and stored or rapidly restored to firing position. To the left are ammunition-box racks. *National Archives*

The position of the starboard waist hatch door when opened is shown, along with a .50-caliber machine gun in its firing position. Small stencils indicate where a ladder was to be hooked over the bottom of the hatch. A retractable post is aft of the hatch. *National Archives*

Aft of the waist compartment in the PBY-1 was a tunnel-gun position, with a .30-caliber machine gun on a swiveling mount called the stirrup (shown here in the stowed position). The gun could be fired through the hatch on the bottom of the hull to the far left. *National Archives*

A .30-caliber machine gun with ring and bead sights is pointing out of the hatch in the tunnel position; the aft part of the hull is to the upper right. When the hatch door was open, it was stowed in a vertical position next to the hatch inside the aircraft. *National Archives*

The number 11 aircraft of Patrol Squadron 12 (VP-12) in 1937 was this PBY-1. The two horizontal stripes on the rudder denoted Patrol Wing (PatWing) 1. National insignia at this stage of the PBY's development were limited to the wings.

PBYs of Patrol Squadron 12, *to the left*, and Patrol Squadron 9, *on the right*, are assembled on the ramp at San Diego in June 1938, prior to taking off on a loose-formation flight to Seattle. Fabric covers are over the cowls and cockpit canopies. *National Museum of Naval Aviation*

PBY-1 BuNo 0135 of VP-12F (redesignated VP-12 on October 1, 1937) is anchored in Lake Washington, near Seattle, in 1937. The number "11" in its markings indicated that it was the second aircraft in the fourth section; there were three aircraft in each section. *National Museum of Naval Aviation*

PBY-1 BuNo 0156 participates in fleet tactical exercises on November 17, 1937. The top of the wing was Chrome Yellow, with a black section in the middle of it. Metal surfaces on the hull were coated with Aluminum paint and fabric surfaces with Aluminum dope. *National Archives*

On April 13, 1937, PBY-1 BuNo 0124 of VP-11F approaches the coast of Oahu near Honolulu, the floats extended preparatory to landing. This was part of a twelve-plane flight that had made the ocean crossing from San Diego under Lt. Cmdr. L. A. Pope. *National Museum of Naval Aviation*

Consolidated Aircraft sold a number of PBYs commercially for civilian and government use. The first such sale was of this Model 28-1, the designation for an unarmed, all-weather PBY-1. The American Museum of Natural History acquired it in early 1937 for one of its research associates, Richard Archbold, to use on a scientific expedition to Dutch New Guinea. Archbold made several shakedown flights in the aircraft, nicknamed Guba after the Papuan word for "fierce storm," but before he was scheduled to leave for Dutch New Guinea, he sold the plane to the Soviets, who planned to employ it in a search for Sigizmund Levanevsky and his expeditionary team, who were lost during a flight over the North Pole on August 13, 1937. Despite an extensive international search effort, Levanevsky and his crew were never located. *National Museum of Naval Aviation*

On July 25, 1936, the US Navy issued a contract for fifty PBY-2s to Consolidated Aircraft. Outwardly, the PBY-2 was virtually identical to the PBY-1, with the exception of a new feature in the empennage: instead of the PBY-1's elevators, which had angled inner edges to give clearance to the rudder, a new horizontal stabilizer was designed with a center section incorporating a complete chord. A cutout in the rudder permitted it to turn to port or starboard over the rear part of the horizontal stabilizer. Redesigned elevators had inboard edges set at right angles to the leading edges of the elevators, and also spaced outboard from the rudder. Seen here is the PBY-2, BuNo 0454, in VP-11F markings in May 1937. *National Archives*

PBY-2 BuNo 0454 rests on a tarmac at Consolidated Aircraft's San Diego plant on May 15, 1937. This model still retained the sliding hatch doors with small windows on top of the hull aft of the wing. A good view is offered of the lowered starboard float. *National Archives*

The engine nacelles and wing pylon of a PBY-2 are highlighted in a May 22, 1937, factory photo. At the bottoms of the nacelles are air intakes for the updraft carburetors. To the left is the starboard oil-cooler air intake. A radio-direction-finding (RDF) loop antenna is to the lower right. *National Archives*

A subassembly of a PBY-2 horizontal stabilizer and elevators and the upper part of the vertical fin illustrates how the center part of the horizontal stabilizer formed a complete airfoil chord, with the inboard edges of the elevators shaped to fit within the stabilizer. *National Archives*

The empennage of the first PBY-2, BuNo 0454, is displayed. From this angle, it is noticeable how the rudder is cut out around the rear center part of the horizontal elevator. This is an important feature in differentiating the PBY-1 from the PBY-2 (and PBY-3). *National Archives*

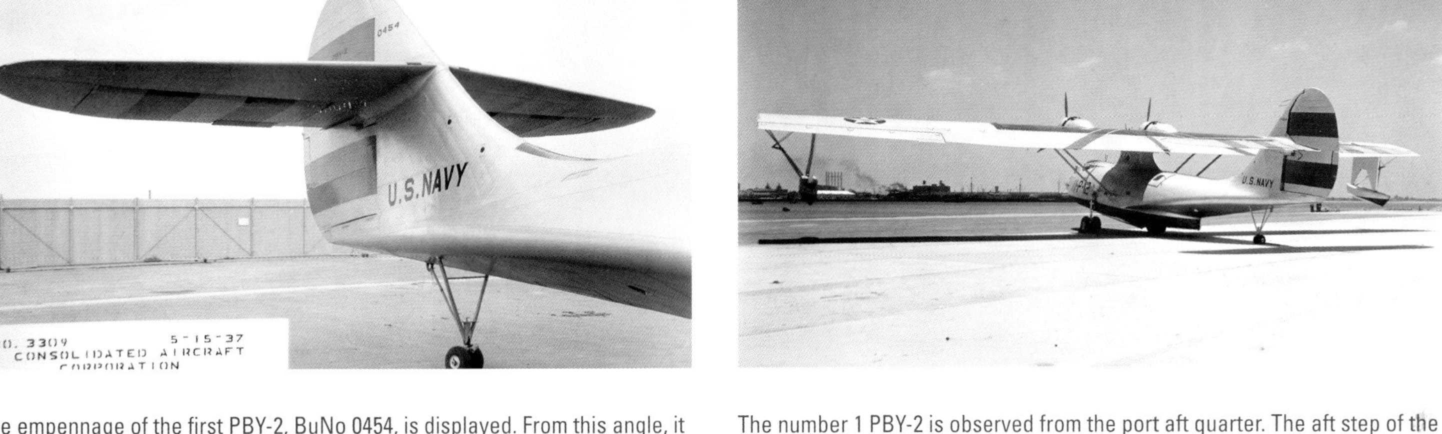

The number 1 PBY-2 is observed from the port aft quarter. The aft step of the hull, the breaker step, which terminates in a V shape forward of the aft beaching gear, is visible. The rear of the forward step, the taper step, is directly below the aft wing struts. *National Archives*

The first PBY-2 is viewed from aft in a May 15, 1937, photograph. Even from this angle, the newly designed horizontal stabilizer and elevators are apparent. Until the advent of the clear bubbles in the waist of later PBYs, visibility to the rear was a problem. *National Archives*

The forward and aft steps of PBY-2 BuNo 0454 are visible. Getting "up on the step" is an essential element of flying-boat design, providing the pilot with a means of achieving minimal friction between the bottom of the hull and the water, ensuring a good takeoff. *National Archives*

At San Diego on May 15, 1937, a photographer captured this frontal view of the first PBY-2. Dominating the front end of the hull is the turret, which obscured the pilot's and copilot's view straight ahead and downward. The ground clearance of the hull is visible. *National Archives*

Engines running, a PBY-2 assigned to duty at NAS Jacksonville, Florida, is being prepared for towing. A crewman is securing a line from the tractor in the background to the tow ring on the underside of the hull, adjacent to the aft beaching gear. *National Museum of Naval Aviation*

The same PBY-2 seen in the preceding photo is being eased down a ramp lined with beaching gears. The beaching gear is still attached to the hull, and the crewmen walking along the aircraft will remove the beaching gear when the aircraft is afloat. *National Museum of Naval Aviation*

While members of the flight crew watch something in the sky, PBY-2 BuNo 0490 rests in water along a shore, a portable ramp alongside it. This flying boat saw much service in Florida, where it experienced at least three accidents between 1940 and 1944. *National Museum of Naval Aviation*

The first US Navy aircraft to be fitted with radar equipment was this PBY-2, BuNo 0456. The plane was at NAS Anacostia in October 1940, conducting tests of the system for the Naval Research Laboratory. Various arrays of antennas are visible on the hull. *American Aviation Historical Society*

After the American Museum of Natural History transferred "Guba" to the Soviet Union, in December 1937 the museum acquired a second flying boat, a PBY-2 nicknamed "Guba II," for Dr. Richard Archbold's scientific expedition to New Guinea. *San Diego Air and Space Museum*

The markings of "Guba II" were virtually identical of the original "Guba." In addition to Archbold's personal insignia, two identifying characteristics of "Guba II" are visible: an RDF "football" antenna atop the wing, and the pitot tube and mast atop the canopy. *San Diego Air and Space Museum*

The first PBY-3, BuNo 0842, takes flight. This model varied from the PBY-2 primarily in the installation of Pratt & Whitney R-1830-66 engines, rated at 900 horsepower, an increase of 50 horsepower over the Pratt & Whitney R-1830-64 used in the PBY-1 and PBY-2. The one noticeable difference of the PBY-3 over the PBY-2 was the intake for the downdraft carburetors, which were on top of the engine nacelles. The US Navy contracted for sixty-six PBY-3s on November 27, 1936; the first one was delivered in November 1937, and the last was delivered in August 1938. *National Museum of Naval Aviation*

Three PBY-3s of VP-41 fly over Cape St. Elias, Alaska Territory, around 1939, displaying the checkerboard tail markings of Patrol Wing (PatWing) 4. This squadron had been redesignated from VP-16 on July 1, 1939, and received its first PBY-3s in June 1938. *National Museum of Naval Aviation*

A PBY-3 taxis in water. The paint scheme appears to have been aluminum, with a yellow wing top with a black walkway area on the wing. Atop the center of the wing is the RDF loop antenna; many PBY-3s had this antenna positioned on top of the cockpit canopy. *Stan Piet collection*

Occasionally, PBYs suffered mishaps during landings and takeoffs on water. This one, assigned to VP-5, suffered a nearly severed tail section, but the wing and its struts are still intact. A floating crane is in the process of salvaging the wreck off San Diego. *San Diego Air and Space Museum*

The port engine nacelle of a PBY-3 is viewed from atop the wing. The cowl panels and cowl flaps have been removed, exposing to view the inner framework of the cowl. Protruding above all is the carburetor air intake, flanked on each side by an engine exhaust port. The round object aft of the carburetor air intake is the access door for the port oil-filler neck and cap. The dark panel at the bottom is a structural inspection door. *National Archives*

A Consolidated Aircraft factory photo from September 1937 shows a torpedo rack and related accessories installed under the starboard side of a PBY-3 wing. The stanchions of portable work platforms are inserted into T-shaped openings on the skin of the wing. *National Archives*

A torpedo director is on the dash above the instrument panel in the cockpit of a PBY-3. It included a simple computing mechanism and provided the pilot with the proper bearings for releasing the torpedo. The pilot or copilot controlled the release of the torpedoes. *National Archives*

At least sixteen PBY-3s are undergoing final assembly at the Consolidated plant in San Diego on February 8, 1938. The first two hulls already have markings for VP-9 below the cockpits. The sixty-six PBY-3s produced were shipped to VP-4, VP-5, VP-9, and VP-16.

Crewman heave on a mooring line attached to the aft tow eye of a PBY-3 at NAS Corpus Christi. To install or remove the beaching gear, to moor the flying boat or secure tow lines to it, to steady the craft, and to perform other tasks, it was necessary for handlers to enter the water. When the water was warm, swimsuits were in order for PBY handlers; when it was cold, wetsuits were worn. The national insignia on this PBY-3 have red circles within the white stars. *Stan Piet collection*

Crewmen at the seaplane ramp at NAS Corpus Christi rig a portable walkway next to a PBY-3, to enable the crew to enter or debark without getting themselves or their equipment wet. The man under the tail is securing a mooring line to the aft tow eye. *Stan Piet collection*

A PBY-3 assigned to VN-4D8, a training squadron at NAS Pensacola, taxis on the water. The plane's number, "91," is in black on each side of the wing. The national insignia are of the type without the red circle in the center, in use from May 1942 to June 1943. *Stan Piet collection*

Three PBY-3s assigned to NAS Corpus Christi fly over the Gulf of Mexico. They wear national insignia of the type in use from May 1942 to June 1943. The wing tops are a shade of yellow, and the hulls are evidently a shade of Non-Specular Blue or Blue Gray. *Stan Piet collection*

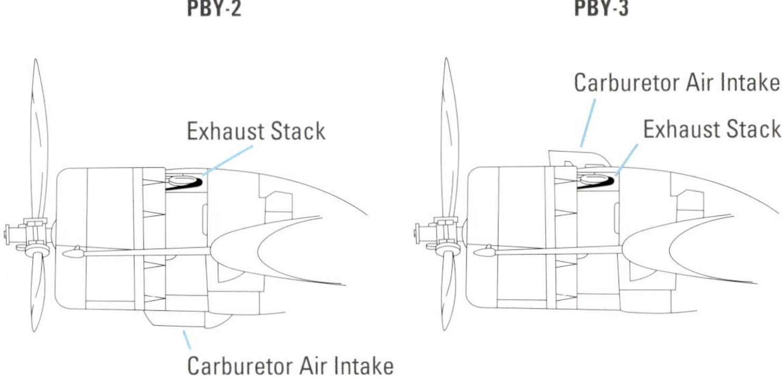

This diagram indicates the key difference between the PBY-2 from the PBY-3: the PBY-2 had an updraft carburetor, with the air intake below the engine nacelle, while the PBY-3 had a downdraft carburetor, with the air intake atop the nacelle between the exhausts.

Consolidated Aircraft and the US Navy inked a contract on December 18, 1937, for thirty-three PBY-4s. The main substantive change in the PBY-4 from the PBY-3 was the new Pratt & Whitney R-1830-72 engine, rated at 1,050 horsepower, an increase of 150 horsepower over the PBY-3's Pratt & Whitney R-1830-66 engines, rated at 900 horsepower. About the only visually discernible difference between the PBY-4 and its immediate predecessor was the addition of propeller spinners, although a small number of PBY-2s and PBY-3s apparently were briefly retrofitted with spinners. Seen here is a PBY-4 assigned to VP-13. *National Museum of Naval Aviation*

Before World War II, the Marine Corps developed a force called the air infantry: assault troops that were transported and landed by aircraft. Members of a USMC air infantry battalion stand with their equipment, with a PBY-4 of VF-12 in the background. *National Archives*

Another group from a USMC air infantry brigade pose for their photograph near the same PBY-4 seen in the preceding photograph. Air infantry troops were distinct from paratroopers in that they rode their aircraft all the way, or close, to their destination. *National Archives*

A member of a USMC air infantry brigade hands an equipment pack to another Marine inside the port waist hatch of a PBY-4 of VP-12 on March 25, 1941. A boarding ladder is attached to the hatch, and the wild-goose insignia of VP-12 is on the side of the hull. Formerly designated VP-9, VP-12 would once again be redesignated on August 1, 1941, as VP-24 and assigned to Patrol Wing 2 at NAS Kaneohe. On October 1, 1941, the squadron was reassigned to NAS Ford Island, in the middle of Pearl Harbor. *National Archives*

A gunner mans the .30-caliber machine gun in the starboard waist hatch of an early-model PBY. On the left side of the gun cradle is a box for the .30-caliber ammunition. The stirrup, the mount that could be swiveled down to store the gun so that the weapon could quickly be brought back into firing position if necessary, is visible below the cradle. Aft of the hatch is a stencil for a pullout snubbing post, used for securing a line to the hull. Stencils indicating the locations for attaching a ladder are below the hatch. *Library of Congress*

On May 2, 1941, a contingent of an air infantry brigade is preparing to board five PBYs, including at least one that appears to be a PBY-4. Neutrality stars are visible on several of the PBYs. To the far right is PBY number "12" of VP-12, seen in several preceding photos. *National Archives*

A PBY carrying a team of air infantry has just entered the water and is preparing for takeoff. An aircrewman wearing a flying helmet and a harness is standing up in the port waist hatch. Several men are in the water, removing the main beaching gear. *National Archives*

A PBY-4 of VP-17 is being prepared for a flight to Sitka, Alaska, in the late fall of 1938. Survival gear has been laid out alongside the flying boat for inspection. Some of the items include life jackets, a VP-17 life ring, bedrolls, thermos bottles, and a cook stove. *National Museum of Naval Aviation*

Several PBYs are on the ramp and in the water at the Naval Torpedo Station, Gould Island Facility, in Narragansett Bay, Rhode Island, in 1939. The plane in the water to the far right has markings for VP-54. The Navy proof-tested its torpedoes at Gould Island. *National Museum of Naval Aviation*

An officer on the ground gives hand signals to the man standing on the starboard engine nacelle of a PBY and straining to hear the officer's orders. This aircraft has the propeller spinners associated with the PBY-4. Numerous fine details are visible on the original print, such as a curved section of rough, nonslip finish on the side of the bow underneath the pendant between the anchor-box door and the front of the chine rail. Where the shadow of the propeller falls on the side of the hull, between the national insignia and the numeral "2," is a thin strip of metal that acted as a shield if the propeller should cast off chunks of ice. This feature dated back to the PBY-2. *Stan Piet collection*

The Transatlantic was a Consolidated Model 28-4, a civilian version of the PBY-4, flown by American Export Lines to investigate potential airline routes from the United States to Europe in 1938. In place of the bow turret, there was a streamlined fairing. *San Diego Air and Space Museum*

The final four PBY-4 aircraft featured improved waist gun positions distinguished by large blisters rather than the sliding hatch. The new style of blister was carried forward into subsequent Catalina production. This is the fourth-from-final PBY-4. *National Museum of Naval Aviation*

Propeller Hub-Spinner Development

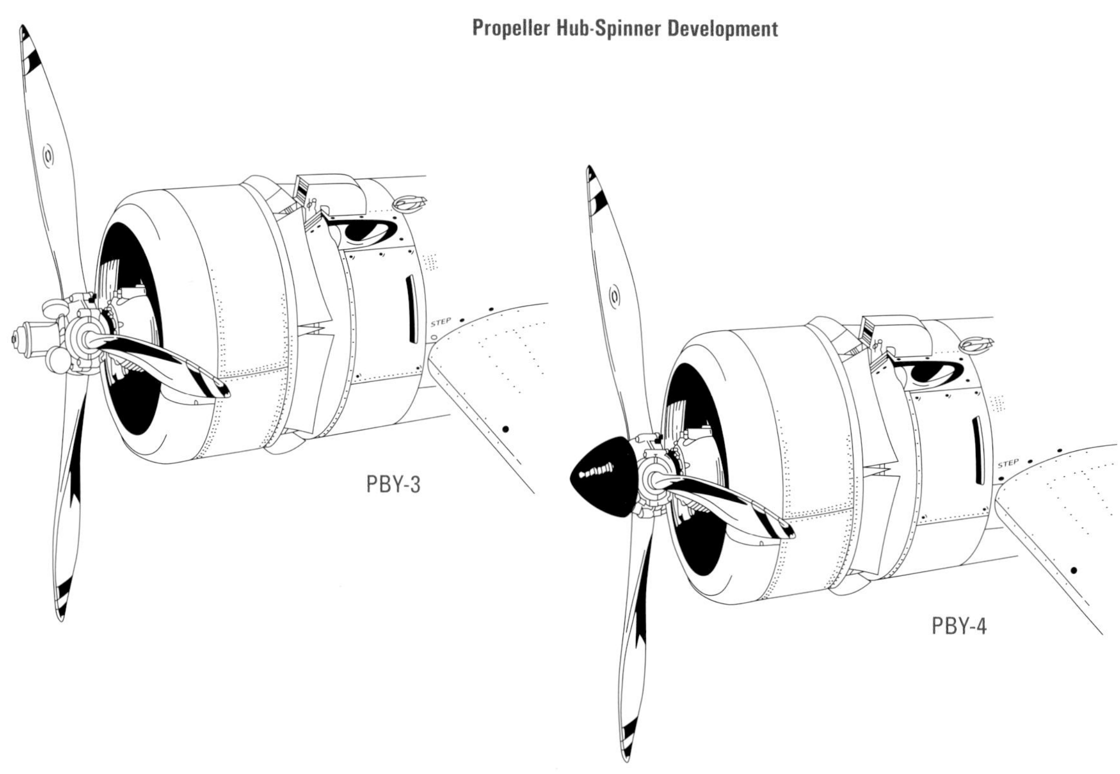

PBYs up to the PBY-3 did not have a spinner over the propeller hub. PBY-4s added a spinner to the propeller, offering a useful identification aid for that model of flying boat. However, a few earlier PBYs are known to have been retrofitted with propeller spinners.

Patrol Squadron 18 was one of the units to receive PBY-4s. This example, number 6 of the squadron, is poised on beaching gear on a ramp at a US Coast Guard station in early March 1939. Aluminum paint is on the wing and hull, with black on the hull bottom. *National Archives*

PBY-5 number 8 of VP-52 is being towed at NAS Norfolk. The PBY-5 reflected modifications that had been made to the last four PBY-4s, including the substitution of clear blisters on each side of the waist for the sliding hatch doors; redesigned engine cowls, rudder, and vertical fin; and oil coolers moved to the bottoms of the engine nacelles. The horizontal stabilizers and elevators were redesigned and enlarged. In yet another power plant upgrade, Pratt & Whitney R-1830-82 engines were installed. *National Museum of Naval Aviation*

The waist blisters of the PBY-5 had a pivoting section in the middle, which, when rolled open, allowed the gunner to point his flexible machine gun out into the open. Here, Ordnanceman Jesse Rhodes Waller mans a Browning M1919 .30-caliber machine gun. *Library of Congress*

US Navy ordnanceman Jesse Waller is viewed from another angle with an M1919 .30-caliber machine gun at NAS Corpus Christi, Texas, in August 1942. The box to the gunner's left holds ammunition; the smaller box to his right collects spent casings. *Library of Congress*

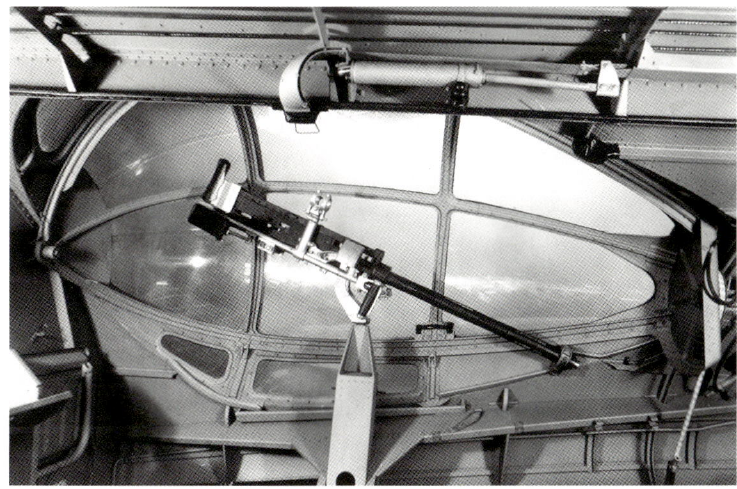

Waist Gunner Position

Waist Gunner's Hatch

Waist Gunner's Blister

PBY-4

PBY-5

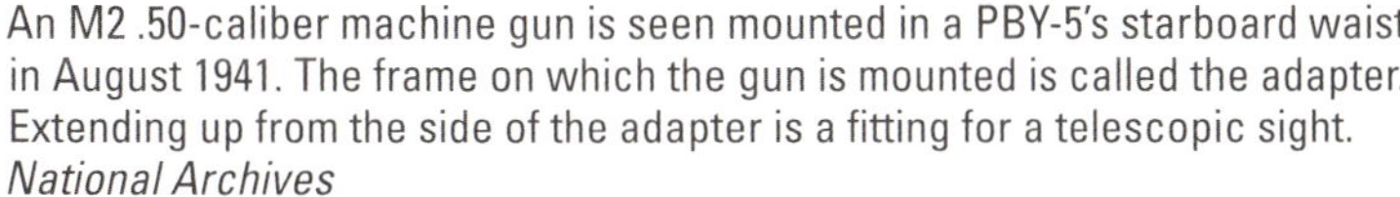

An M2 .50-caliber machine gun is seen mounted in a PBY-5's starboard waist in August 1941. The frame on which the gun is mounted is called the adapter. Extending up from the side of the adapter is a fitting for a telescopic sight. *National Archives*

With the PBY-5, the sliding hatches in the waist of preceding models of PBY were eliminated in favor of large blisters with Plexiglas windows and metal frames. These blisters provided the waist gunners with a much-greater field of vision.

The number 6 PBY-5 of Patrol Squadron 52 rests on the ramp at NAS Quonset Point, Rhode Island, on March 26, 1941. The hull and the bottom of the wing were painted aluminum, with a thin black band around the hull at the waterline. *National Museum of Naval Aviation*

A PBY-5 sits on a ramp on April 29, 1941, providing a three-quarters rear view from its port side. A crew access ladder is hanging from the side of the hull, adjacent to the port blister. A neutrality star with red circle in the center is visible on the hull adjacent to the cockpit. *National Archives*

This PBY-5 was photographed on the occasion of the first visit of a PBY to the seaplane base at Crescent Harbor, Washington, in December 1942. A close inspection of the photo discloses that under the wing are Yagi radar antennas, bomb racks, and torpedo racks. *Tracy White collection*

As on preceding models of the PBY, the PBY-5 canopy had sliding hatch doors. Inside the copilot's hatch, a torpedo director is visible below the forward inboard corner of the hatch. Attached to the pilot's control wheel is the aileron and elevator locking bar. *National Archives*

An officer and the copilot of a PBY-5 of VP-51 exchange a document. The aircraft has the Non-Specular Blue Gray and Non-Specular Light Gray camouflage scheme and a neutrality star. The RDF loop antenna is barely visible behind the propeller blade. *National Museum of Naval Aviation*

Tail Development

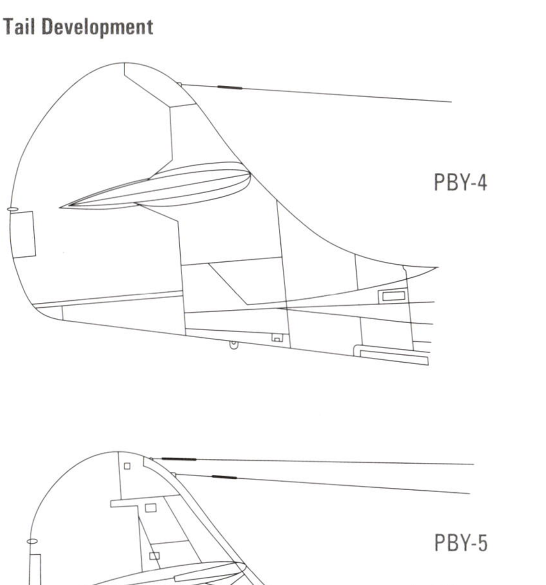

DF Loop Development

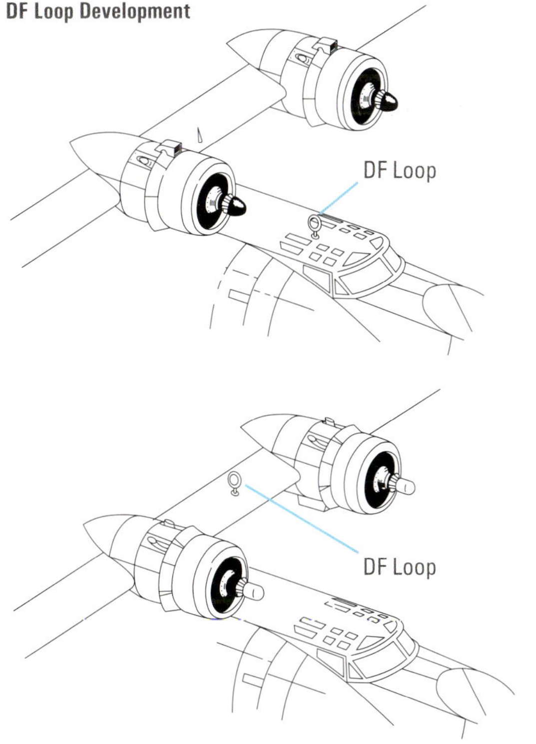

Changes were made in the vertical fin and rudder of the PBY-5, resulting in a straighter trailing edge for the rudder. The RDF loop antenna was moved from the cockpit canopy on the PBY-4 to the top of the center section of the wing on the PBY-5.

Seen here from the starboard side, this PBY-5 is most likely painted in Non-Specular Blue Gray on the upper surfaces and sides of the hull and the top of the wing, and Non-Specular Light Gray on the undersides of the hull and wing. *National Archives*

An "eyeball" turret, a late type of PBY bow turret with a bulging Plexiglas window at the front, has been fitted on this PBY-5; the turret is traversed toward the starboard. White bars have been added to the sides of the national insignia, a measure instituted in 1943. *National Museum of Naval Aviation*

Three PBY-5s fly in formation over a shoreline. They have neutrality stars with red circles and are painted in the scheme of Non-Specular Blue Gray on the tops and sides of the hull and the tops of the wing, and Non-Specular Light Gray on the bottom surfaces. *Stan Piet collection*

PBY-5s assigned to VPB-2 at NAS Jacksonville, Florida, fly in formation on April 17, 1945. Variations are visible in the paint schemes of the three Catalinas; for example, the second and third planes have light-colored pylons, which the first plane lacks. *National Museum of Naval Aviation*

Preparations are underway to beach a PBY-5, unit/aircraft code J1-P-11. The man in the water to the front of the aircraft is giving directions to the pilot for proper positioning. Once the plane shuts down its engines, beaching gear will be installed. *Stan Piet collection*

In a continuation of the scene in the preceding photograph, the PBY-5 is being prepared for towing, tail first, up the seaplane ramp. Fortunately for the beaching crew, the water is warm, and they can wear swimsuits while attaching the beaching gear and tow lines. *Stan Piet collection*

Beaching crews were not always as lucky as those in the preceding photo. This crew has donned wetsuits prior to getting into the water to retrieve a PBY-5. Lines are attached to the hull, aft of the starboard blister, inside of which several aircrewmen are standing by. *Stan Piet collection*

The beaching gear has been installed, the swimmers of the beaching crew are clearing the water, and an Oliver tractor is making ready to tow the PBY-5 out of the water and up the ramp. One of the PBY's crewmen is watching the proceedings from atop the wing. *National Museum of Naval Aviation*

A beaching crew tends a PBY-5 while a tractor waits on the ramp. The aircraft appears to be finished in a Royal Air Force (RAF) camouflage scheme, with the top of the wing and the fuselage above the waterline painted Extra Dark Sea Grey and Dark Slate Grey, with Sky below the waterline. *Stan Piet collection*

The British and Commonwealth countries flew various models of the PBY, including PBY-5s designated as Catalina I. Here, a Royal Australian Air Force Catalina I, registration number A24-18, is on a ramp. It was shot down near Bougainville in May 1942. *San Diego Air and Space Museum*

RAF Catalinas fly on a mission. Catalinas served the RAF well during the Battle of the Atlantic, patrolling the sea lanes. *National Museum of Naval Aviation*

An RAF Catalina I flies over a spit of land. The British began receiving Catalinas in late 1940. A typical camouflage scheme for RAF Catalinas was Extra Dark Sea Grey and Dark Slate Grey, with Sky on the bottom of the hull and the bottom of the wing. *San Diego Air and Space Museum*

This Catalina I located and followed the German battleship *Bismarck* on May 26, 1941. The aircraft, SN W8406 WQ-Z, flew with RAF's 209 Squadron. The pilot was Dennis Briggs, and the copilot was Ens. Leonard Smith, one of a few US Navy personnel sent to England to train PBY crews. *Bismarck* fired on—and hit—but did not down the PBY, making it the first Catalina to draw fire.

Royal Canadian Air Force (RCAF) Canso 9706 appears to have been painted overall in aluminum paint, with a thin black band around the hull at the waterline level. The Royal Canadian Air Force operated PBYs under the name Canso, including this PBY-5, which was delivered on September 8, 1941. *San Diego Air and Space Museum*

As Canso 9706 flies above a shoreline, the pitot tube on the port side of the wing appears to be a British type, with the static sensor offset below the mast. In addition to the USAF and RCAF, the RAF, the Royal Australian Air Force, and the Royal New Zealand Air Force all flew versions of the PBY. *San Diego Air and Space Museum*

PBY-5 BuNo 2360 was assigned to VP-14 at NAS Kaneohe, Oahu, at the time of the December 7, 1941, Japanese attack. It is shown in the colors and markings it bore from January to May 1942. The basic finish scheme was blue gray over light gray.

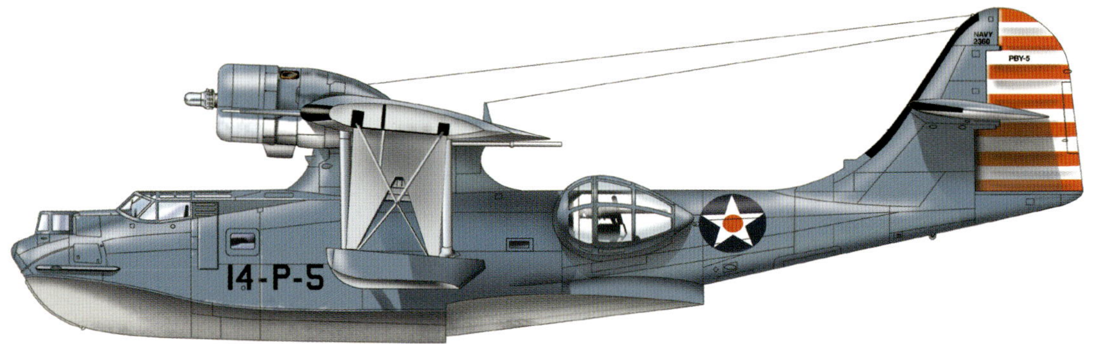

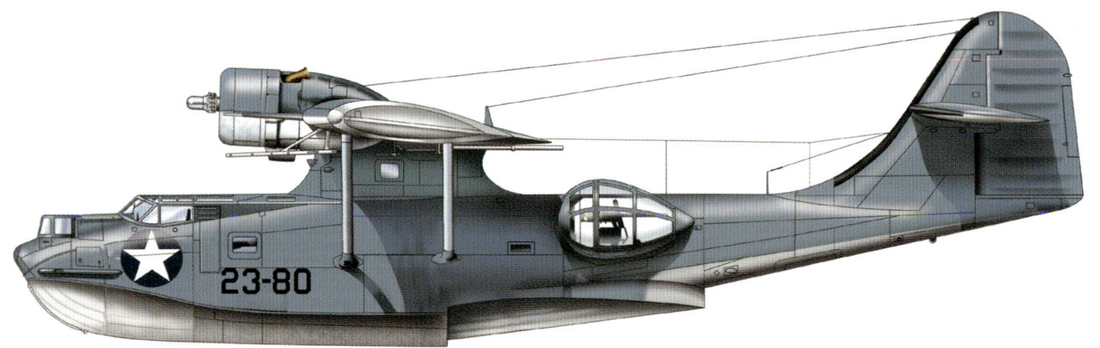

PBY-5 of VP-23 appears as it did in the Pacific theater of operations in 1943. The upper part of the wing and the top and sides of the hull were painted blue gray, and the bottom of the wing and the bottom of the hull were light gray. Yagi arrays are below the wings.

One can almost imagine this museum PBY-5 taking off into flight from a water surface. The paint of US Navy Catalinas in World War II would not have been glossy, as on this example.

The pendant (the cable essential to the anchor system) is in its proper position, running from the anchor compartment along the chine rail and down the front of the keel on this rare PBY-5, on display at the National Museum of Naval Aviation. PBY-5 aircraft lack the nose landing-gear doors of the later PBY-5A. *Author*

In addition to the mechanic's window in the wing pylon and the small window forward of the blister, this PBY-5 has a small window between the wing struts, a feature found on some PBY-5s. The pipe is a fuel jettison tube. *Author*

In this view of the starboard midsection of a PBY-5, the door of the blister is open, offering a view of the .50-caliber machine gun and its armor shield. This side of the aircraft lacks the small window between the wing struts. *Author*

As viewed from below and aft, both steps of the hull of a PBY-5 are in view, with the aft step at the top of the photo and the forward step toward the bottom. *Author*

CHAPTER 2

The Amphibians

Up to this point, all the Catalinas had been true flying boats, requiring beaching gear to come ashore. Now, however, it was considered advantageous for the airplane to be an amphibian, and thus able to operate from either water or land. Accordingly, the last production PBY-4, Bureau Number (BuNo) 1245, was outfitted with retractable landing gear, becoming the XPBY-5A. The aircraft was first flown in this configuration on November 22, 1939.

The Navy was so pleased with the results of this version that a contract modification specified that the last thirty-three PBY-5 aircraft on order were to be completed as PBY-5A aircraft instead. Deliveries of these planes began in October 1941. Beyond these thirty-three aircraft, on November 25, 1940, the Navy had ordered a further 134 PBY-5As. Deliveries of those aircraft began in December 1941.

Following the Japanese attack on Pearl Harbor, 635 more PBY-5A aircraft were ordered from Consolidated by the Navy. However, some of these were delivered to Australia, Britain, Canada, and the Free French, in addition to the US Army. In Army service, they were designated OA-10.

Boeing of Canada also began producing this aircraft during 1940, and it was joined by Canadian Vickers. Two hundred thirty of the latter were delivered to the US Army Air Force, where they were referred to as OA-10A. However, the Royal Canadian Air Force in December 1941 decreed that the Canadian-built aircraft, owing to differences with their US-built counterparts, would not be referred to as Catalinas. Rather, the name to be used was Canso—referencing the Strait of Canso, which separates Nova Scotia from Cape Breton Island. PBY-5A aircraft were to be referred to as Canso As.

As production of the PBY-5A progressed, various changes were introduced, including the installation of a search radar above the cockpit, and an improved bow machine gun turret.

The PBY-5A was superseded by the PBY-6A, which had an improved tail design. Orders were placed for nine hundred of these aircraft to be built at Consolidated's New Orleans plant, but when Germany surrendered in May 1945, the order was canceled. Only 175 of the PBY-6As had been completed. Seventy-five of those went to the US Army under the designation OA-10B, and forty-eight were supplied to the Soviet Union. The PBY-6A was the last of the Catalinas built by Consolidated, whose total production of the type was 2,398 aircraft. A further nine hundred were built by Boeing of Canada, Canadian Vickers, and the Naval Aircraft Factory. The USSR built an unknown number of duplicates called GST.

Following World War II, the US Navy quickly retired its Catalina flying boats, but the amphibious Catalinas continued to serve for many years. Finally, the US Navy retired its last Catalina, BuNo 64097, a PBY-6A operating from Naval Air Station Atlanta, in January 1957.

Shown on December 7, 1939, the final PBY-4, BuNo 1244, was developed into the XPBY-5A, the prototype for the PBY-5A. The XPBY-5A lacked the two waist blisters that were hallmarks of both the PBY-5 and -5A but included the retractable tricycle landing gear that was a key feature of the PBY-5A. The landing gear could be used for emergency landings on prepared runways or could be used to beach the aircraft. Provisions were still included for mounting detachable beaching gear in situations where the use of that gear was necessary or desired. *National Archives*

The XPBY-5A retained the PBY-4's rudder with the curved trailing edge and sliding hatches in the waist compartment. Consolidated Aircraft conducted the initial flight of the XPBY-5A on November 22, 1939, and delivered the plane to the Navy the following month. *National Museum of Naval Aviation*

The port main landing gear is lowered and the beaching gear is attached on the XPBY-5A in a December 7, 1939, photo. Tests showed that the retractable landing gear acted as a sea anchor when the aircraft was on water, making it easier to control during beaching. *National Archives*

A view documenting the XPBY-5A, with the main beaching gear on ramps and the bow in the air, provides details of the nose landing gear and doors as well as the retractable metal cover over the bombardier's window. The anchor is hanging by the bow. Above the chine of the hull, on each side of the hull is a chine rail, used for securing lines as well as providing a walkway for crewmen when casting out the anchor, securing mooring lines, and performing other tasks. The engine cowls and nacelles retain characteristics of the PBY-4. It appears that the main landing gear are not fitted in this photo, and rather beaching gear is used on the fuselage. *National Archives*

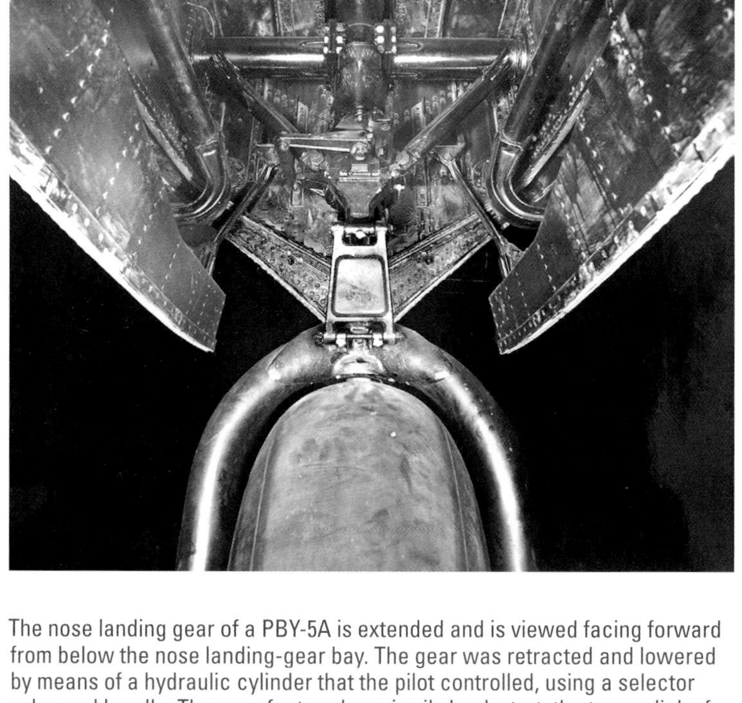

The nose landing gear of a PBY-5A is extended and is viewed facing forward from below the nose landing-gear bay. The gear was retracted and lowered by means of a hydraulic cylinder that the pilot controlled, using a selector valve and handle. The gear featured an air-oil shock strut, the torque link of which is visible above the tire. The tire was a smooth-contour type. The landing gear was provided with automatic locks that activated at the end of the retraction process and unlocked at the beginning of the lowering process. *National Archives*

In an October 21, 1941, photograph of the port main landing gear of a PBY-5A, a jack is rigged to the beaching-gear fittings to the left. The main landing gear was operated by two hydraulic cylinders: a main cylinder and a smaller one. Above the tire is the top of the oleo strut. The diagonal tube from the top of the oleo strut to the upper interior of the landing-gear bay is the main strut. Two V-struts, one over the other, form a linkage from the oleo strut to the lower part of the landing-gear bay. A disk cover is over the wheel. *National Archives*

The wheel of the starboard main landing gear of this PBY-5A lacks the cover seen in the preceding photograph. On the oleo strut above the tire is a folding door that covered the top of the landing-gear bay when the gear was retracted. Goodrich smooth-contour 47-inch tires were specified for the PBY-5A. The tread of the main landing gear, the distance between the centers of the tires, was 16 feet, 9 inches. To the right, on the chine and at the bottom of the wing strut, are fittings for the beaching gear. *National Archives*

The starboard beaching gear is installed on a PBY-5A in a November 1941 photograph. The design was the same as that used on earlier models of the PBY, with long, L-shaped pins securing the strut to a bracket on the chine of the hull, and the top of the strut secured in a fitting in the fairing at the bottom of the forward wing strut. Between the tires is a hand-brake lever. The wheels were Hayes 11.00 × 12 mounting Goodrich 11.00 × 12 smooth-contour, low-pressure tires with Goodrich inner tubes. *National Archives*

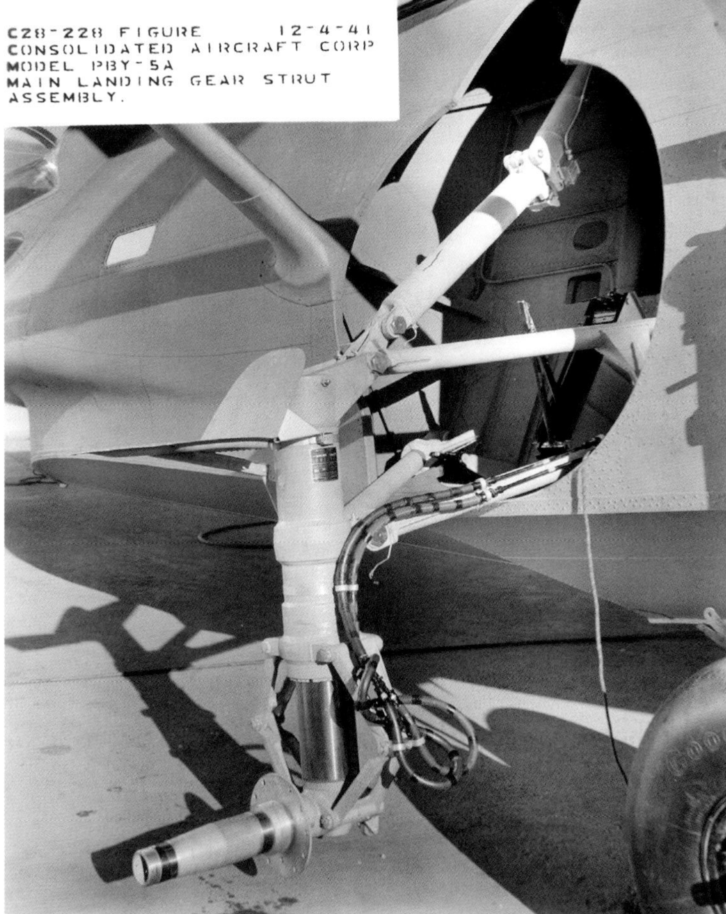

With the wheel removed from the starboard main landing gear of a PBY-5A, the complex system of struts and actuating cylinders is visible. At the bottom of the Cleveland Pneumatic Tool Co. oleo strut is the axle. Antitorque links are positioned at the front and at the rear of the oleo strut. Flexible hydraulic lines are routed from the landing-gear bay along the oleo strut and forward antitorque link. At the center of the landing-gear bay is an oval window that allowed inspection of the landing gear from within the plane. *National Archives*

The instrument panel in the cockpit of the PBY-5A was fairly sparse. The control yoke, fitted with control wheels and electrical switch panels, as seen in previous models of the PBY, was still present. Landing-gear brake pedals were now atop the rudder pedals. *National Archives*

In a view of the instrument panel and control yoke and wheels of the XPBY-5A, the door in the canvas curtain that provided access to and from the bombardier's compartment is secured shut. The rudder pedals lacked the landing-gear brake pedals found on PBY-5As. *National Archives*

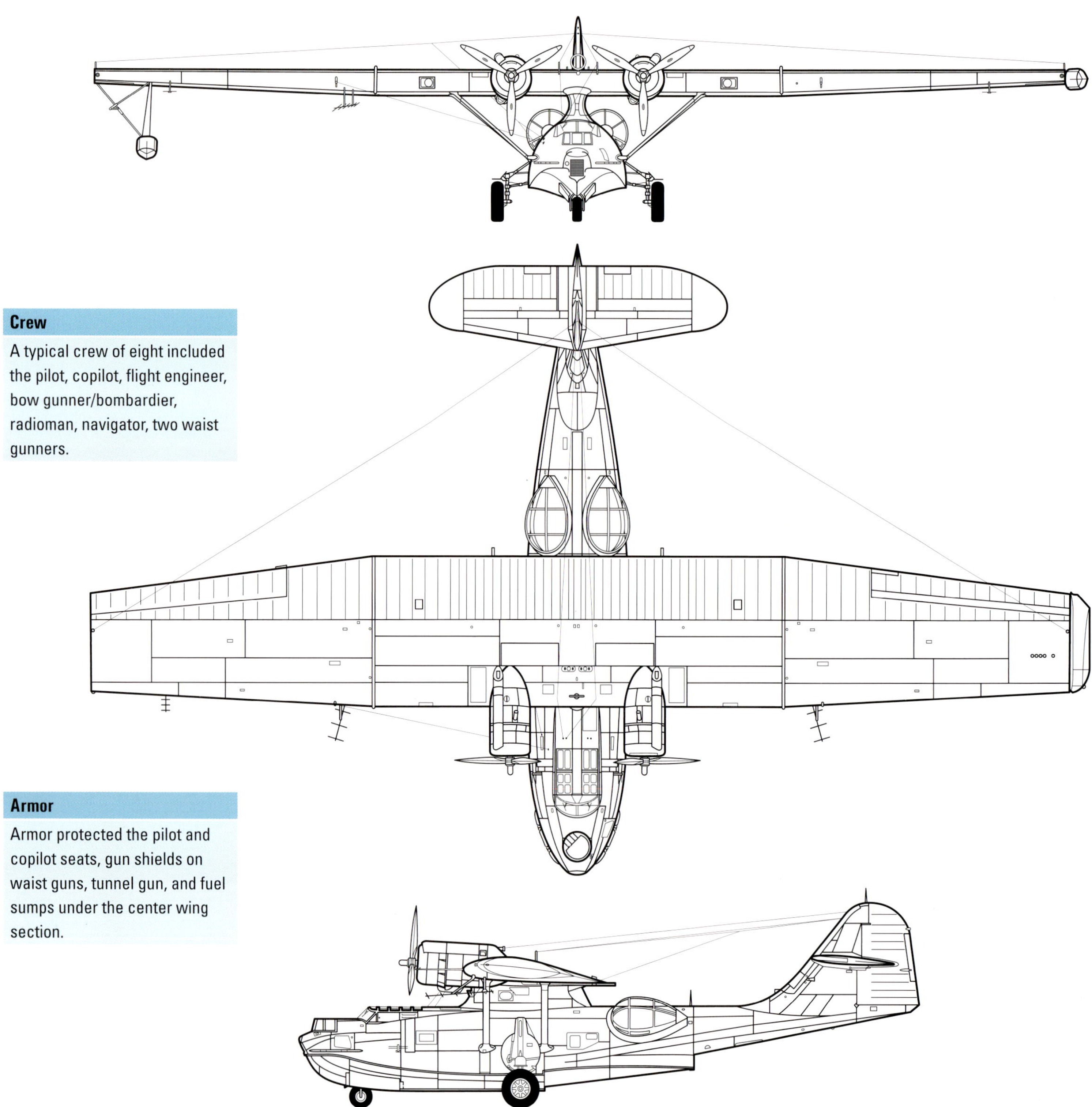

Crew

A typical crew of eight included the pilot, copilot, flight engineer, bow gunner/bombardier, radioman, navigator, two waist gunners.

Armor

Armor protected the pilot and copilot seats, gun shields on waist guns, tunnel gun, and fuel sumps under the center wing section.

drawing—see label guide for additional info

The waist blisters that became standard with the PBY-5 gave late Catalinas a decided advantage over the earlier models in terms of better field of fire for the waist machine guns and better visibility for the waist gunners, who also served as observers. The blisters had a stationary element, the forward part of which served as a windscreen, as seen on this installation in a PBY-5A. The blisters also had an inner, swiveling section that, when rotated upward, provided an opening for firing the machine gun or for entering and exiting the flying boat. Also in view is a plethora of communications wire antennas. *Stan Piet collection*

A close-up of a starboard blister machine gun mount shows the armored shield from the side. The two aluminum-colored tubes to the sides of the pintle mount of the gun are part of the adapter, the shock-buffered frame that the machine gun was mounted on. *Stan Piet collection*

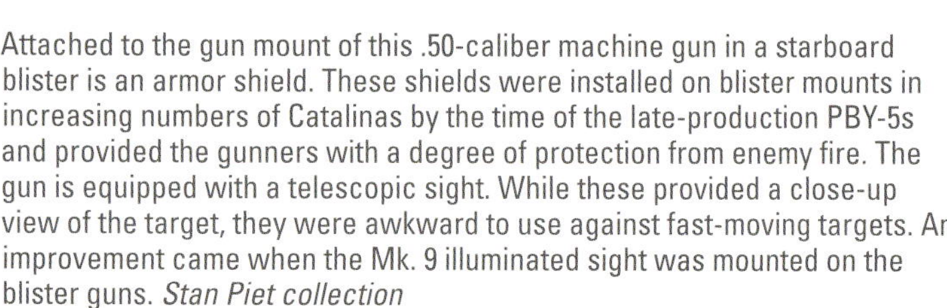

Attached to the gun mount of this .50-caliber machine gun in a starboard blister is an armor shield. These shields were installed on blister mounts in increasing numbers of Catalinas by the time of the late-production PBY-5s and provided the gunners with a degree of protection from enemy fire. The gun is equipped with a telescopic sight. While these provided a close-up view of the target, they were awkward to use against fast-moving targets. An improvement came when the Mk. 9 illuminated sight was mounted on the blister guns. *Stan Piet collection*

A waist gunner mans a Browning M2 .50-caliber machine gun in the starboard window of a PBY-5A. The .50-caliber machine gun, which boasted better stopping power than the .30-caliber machine guns used in early-model PBYs, was commonly used in blister mounts in the later PBYs. On the right side of the gun is a box for .50-caliber ammunition. On the lower part of the blister are two elongated windows, which gave the gunner the bit of extra visibility that could prove crucial during a patrol mission or a defensive air battle. *Stan Piet collection*

A May 15, 1942, Consolidated factory photo shows a .50-caliber machine gun in its stored position inside the starboard blister of a PBY-5A. An armored shield is fitted; the stencils on it instructed the installers which way the two plates of the shield were to face. *National Archives*

A starboard blister machine gun installation is viewed facing aft in a May 15, 1942, photograph. Inboard and above the gun is the movable part of the blister, in its raised position. To the left is the aft pivoting mount for the movable section of the blister. *National Archives*

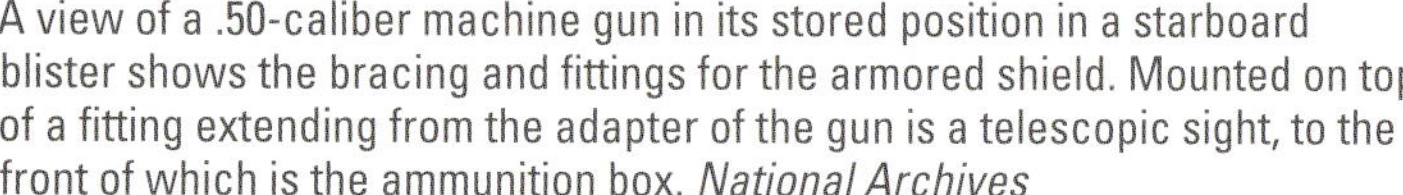

A view of a .50-caliber machine gun in its stored position in a starboard blister shows the bracing and fittings for the armored shield. Mounted on top of a fitting extending from the adapter of the gun is a telescopic sight, to the front of which is the ammunition box. *National Archives*

A waist gunner clad in flying helmet, goggles, and leather flight jacket peers into the telescopic sight of the .50-caliber machine gun. A yellow-colored cushioned eyepiece protected the gunner's eye from sudden shocks and sealed out light and glare. *Stan Piet collection*

Looking into the hull of a PBY-5A aft of the waist machine gun compartment, the tunnel machine gun is in its stowed position at the center. To the right is a flare chute, with a placard giving instructions for loading flares into the swiveling can of the chute. *National Archives*

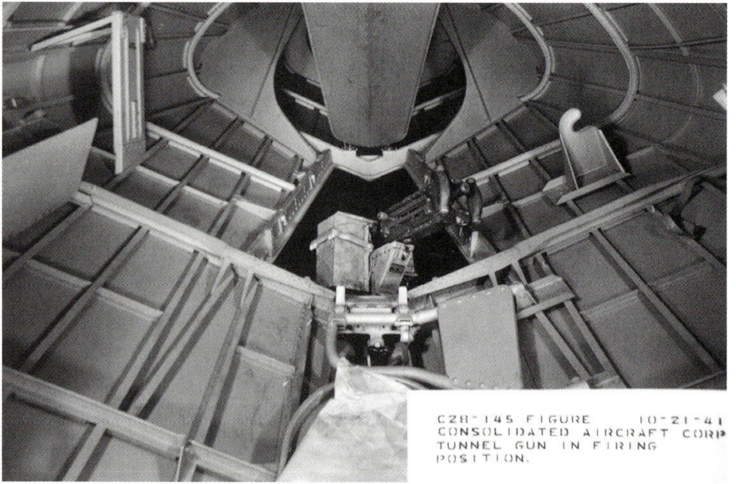

An October 1941 Consolidated Aircraft factory photo shows the tunnel machine gun in its firing position. To the right of the tunnel opening is the stowage bracket for the barrel of the machine gun. Above the gun is the open door for the tunnel opening. *National Archives*

The tunnel gun of a PBY-5A is viewed from the exterior starboard side of the hull. Aft of the ammunition box, the pintle mount of the gun is inserted into the stirrup, the swinging bracket that acts as the gun's support in the firing and the stored positions. *National Archives*

A radio operator makes an adjustment to a RU-19 radio receiver, his other hand poised above a typewriter, at his station aft of the cockpit. He is facing toward the starboard side of the compartment; to the right is the door leading into the mechanic's compartment. *Stan Piet collection*

The bow turret, as shown on a PBY-5A in a late 1941 photograph, had remained virtually unchanged since the PBY-1. The turret top has been removed, revealing the frame, which was of substantial construction. The .50-caliber machine gun is in firing position. *National Archives*

A small armor plate with a sighting hole cut through it is mounted atop the receiver of the .50-caliber machine gun in a PBY-5A bow turret. Another armor plate is below the ring mount to the front of the receiver. A small window is on each side of the turret roof. *National Archives*

A November 1941 view into a PBY-5A bow turret shows the .30-caliber machine gun in its stored position, seeming proportionally small because of the wide-angle lens used. Below are ammunition racks and the bombardier's kneeling pad and inner window cover. *National Archives*

A gunner grasps the handles of an experimental twin Browning M1919 .30-caliber machine gun mount in a PBY bow turret. The guns are mounted with their ammunition feeds on the outboard sides, and a ring-and-bead sight is attached to the installation. *National Archives*

The same twin Browning M1919 .30-caliber machine gun installation depicted in the preceding photograph is viewed from above and aft. The detachable hard top for the turret is not installed. The ammunition boxes on each side of the mount are visible. *National Archives*

A new bow turret was developed toward the end of PBY production. Known as the "eyeball" turret because of the round Plexiglas dome through which twin .30-caliber machine guns protruded, it was introduced starting with PBY-5A BuNo 46580. *National Archives*

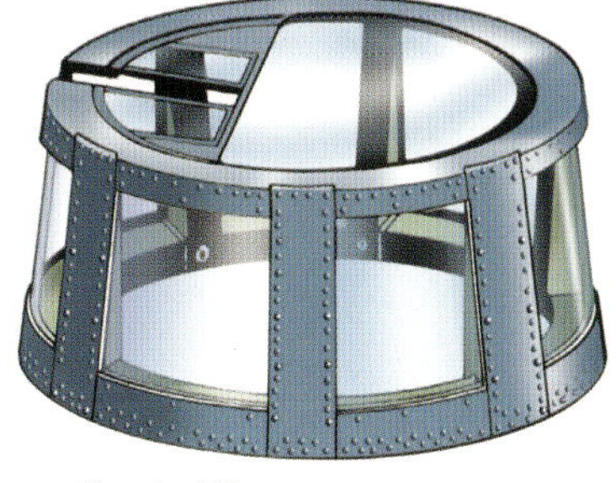

Eyeball Turret

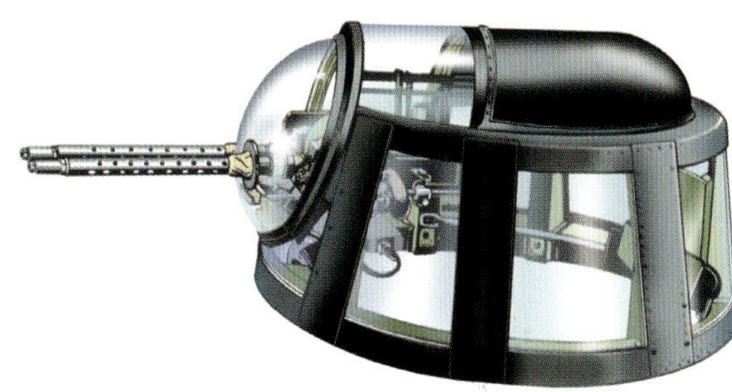

The eyeball turret is viewed from the front. The clear dome flexed with the movement of the machine guns. Contrary to some accounts, the entire turret could be traversed as well. A radome, a late PBY-5A and PBY-6A feature, is visible above the cockpit canopy. *National Archives*

A view from another angle of the eyeball turret shows the twin .30-caliber machine guns fully depressed. Another visible feature is the triangular bombardier's window, a feature of late PBY-5As produced at Consolidated's New Orleans plant, and of PBY-6As. *National Archives*

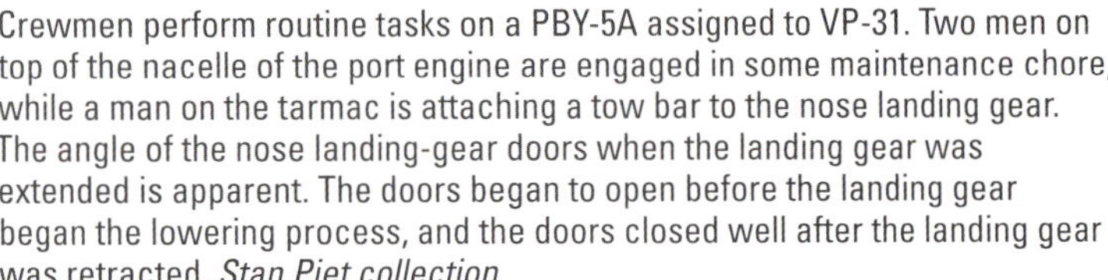
Crewmen perform routine tasks on a PBY-5A assigned to VP-31. Two men on top of the nacelle of the port engine are engaged in some maintenance chore, while a man on the tarmac is attaching a tow bar to the nose landing gear. The angle of the nose landing-gear doors when the landing gear was extended is apparent. The doors began to open before the landing gear began the lowering process, and the doors closed well after the landing gear was retracted. *Stan Piet collection*

Mechanics work on components in the nacelle of the port engine of a VP-31 Catalina. At least one nacelle panel aft of the open cowl flaps has been removed, and the men are preparing to remove another one. To the rear of the man to the left, on the front of the pylon is a feature introduced with the PBY-5A: a beak-like step built into the front of the pylon, which made it easier for crewmen to climb onto the wing from the deck aft of the cockpit canopy. *Stan Piet collection*

Another view of the number 8 flying boat of VP-31 shows the mechanics performing maintenance on elements inside the starboard engine nacelle. A Yagi antenna is in view underneath the port side of the wing, and a ZA blind-landing antenna is on the pitot tube. *Stan Piet collection*

A radome is present over the cockpit of a PBY-5A. Radomes replaced the earlier Yagi radar antennas on late-production PBY-5As and continued to be a feature on the PBY-6A. A protective cover is lashed over the canopy and the eyeball turret. *National Archives*

Although PBYs served in Alaska before World War II, after the Japanese invasion of the Aleutian Islands in June 1942, PBYs played a greater role in patrolling the region's vast expanses. Living conditions were basic, as seen in this view of PBY-5As at a base. *National Archives*

PBY aircrews and ground crews in the Aleutians had to contend with horrendous conditions, with mud, snow, and ice frequently being the norm. Here, a crew at Amchitka Island is securing a PBY-5A during a storm. Depth charges are mounted under the wing. *National Archives*

A fuel truck is servicing a PBY-5A in the Aleutians. The hull is severely splattered with mud. Yagi homing-receiver arrays are visible below each side of the wing, and four bombs are mounted. The code P-1 is painted in black on the side of the hull. *National Archives*

PBY-5As are assembled at a base in the Aleutian Islands. Catalinas of Patrol Wing 4 were on the front lines of the US defenses against the Japanese invasion. The wing had begun receiving PBY-5As in late January 1942 and radar sets for the aircraft that March. *Stan Piet collection*

A PBY-5A awaits its next mission at an airfield in the Aleutian Islands on November 1, 1943. On underwing racks are two general-purpose bombs and two depth charges, a typical mix of ordnance, and the bomb cart in the foreground holds another such load. *Naval History and Heritage Command*

A PBY-5A photographed at an Aleutians airfield bears the US national insignia authorized from late June 1943 to mid-September 1943, with a red border around the blue circle and white wings of the insignia. A ladder is attached aft of the blister. *Stan Piet collection*

Against a backdrop of snowy hills, a PBY-5A of VP-61 conducts a patrol in the Aleutian Islands in March 1943. At that time, the squadron was based at Naval Air Facility (NAF) Otter Point on Umnak Island, with a detachment at NAF Dutch Harbor. *Stan Piet collection*

Although ungainly, slow, and developed for the unglamorous role of maritime patrol, the PBY Catalina was a durable, dependable, and versatile flying boat. This PBY-5A was photographed off the Aleutian Islands. *Stan Piet collection*

The climate of the Aleutian Islands includes extended periods of heavy rainfall and fog, which hampered aviation operations. As a PBY-5A makes a landing on the dirt runway at Amchitka in January 1943, it stirs up a tremendous blast of churning mud. *National Museum of Naval Aviation*

At NAS Dutch Harbor in the Aleutian Islands, a PBY-5A reposes in a revetment created by cutting a gouge into the base of Mount Ballyhoo. As usual for Aleutians-based PBYs, Yagi radar arrays are mounted under the wing, and deicer boots are installed. *Tracy White collection*

As a guard armed with a Thompson submachine gun watches warily to the right, German POWs, survivors of *U-164*, disembark from a PBY-5A of VP-83 that has delivered them to NAS Natal, Brazil, in February 1943. Depth charges are under each side of the wing. *National Museum of Naval Aviation*

With USS *Wichita* in the background, a PBY-5A is being ferried on the deck of the Curtiss-class seaplane tender USS *Albemarle* (AV-5) in a storm off Hvalfjörður, western Iceland, on January 15, 1942. *Albemarle* measured winds of 82 mph that day. *National Archives*

Two stalwarts of US Navy patrol operations in the Battle of the Atlantic cross paths in 1944: an airship and a PBY-5A of VPB-63. Airships were an important factor in the Navy's antisubmarine operations, patrolling and escorting convoys near the US coast. *National Museum of Naval Aviation*

Crewmen on the bow of a PBY-5A are exiting through the copilot's hatch and the top of the bow turret. Another crewman hunkers down on top of the hull between the waist blisters. As can be seen, the chine rails provided just enough surface for a walkway. *National Museum of Naval Aviation*

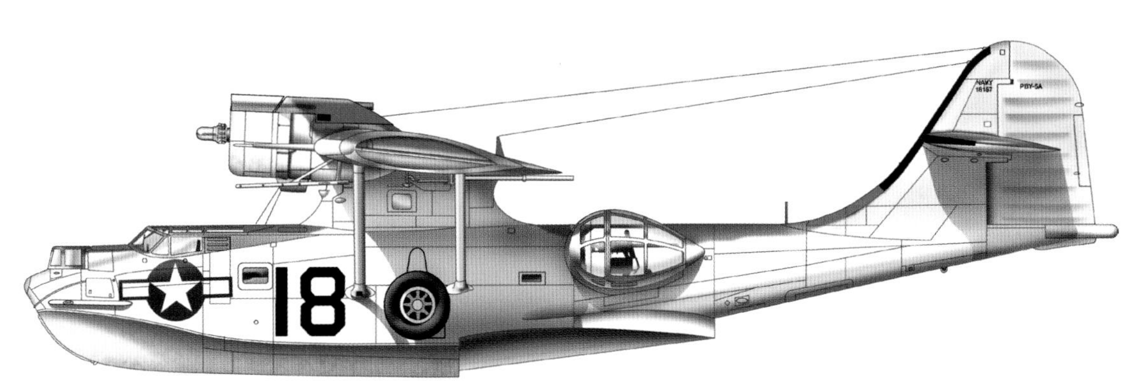

A PBY-5A serving with VPB-63 in 1944 displays the Scheme-2 camouflage scheme developed for USN forces engaged in antisubmarine operations in the Atlantic. It comprised Dark Gull Gray on the top surfaces and Insignia White on the rest.

The step protruding from the front of the wing pylon on a PBY-5A is recognizable in this original wartime color photo. Details of the turret and canopy frames, the Hamilton Standard propellers, and the Pratt & Whitney R-1830-92 engines are also visible. *Stan Piet collection*

Mechanics work on the port blister of a Catalina. The blister hatches were equipped with an inflatable gasket, connected to a hand pump, which sealed off the gap between the swiveling door and the hatch when the door was closed, keeping out drafts and water. *Stan Piet collection*

A view of crewmen performing maintenance on a PBY-5A with a bomb service truck in the foreground also offers copious details of the bottom of the wing, the starboard landing light in the leading edge of the wing, the wing struts, and the engine nacelles and cowls. *Stan Piet collection*

A "Black Cat" PBY-5A is almost touching the water in New Georgia in 1943. The "Black Cats" were PBY squadrons that specialized in night patrol, artillery spotting, and attack missions. The first such squadron was VP-12 on Guadalcanal in 1942. *Stan Piet collection*

Four PBY-5 or PBY-5A "Black Cats" from an unidentified squadron are flying over the Pacific on a patrol mission on May 8, 1944. All four Catalinas are equipped with "eyeball" turrets, and Yagi radar antennas under the wings. *NARA via Dana Bell*

During a takeoff from a base in the South Pacific on May 15, 1944, a PBY-5 or -5A "Black Cat" is on the step "Somewhere in South Pacific, May 15, 1944." Unlike the original bow turret, whose top was level with the deck to the front of the cockpit windshield, the "eyeball" turret's top was noticeably taller than the deck, and this feature is discernible here. *NARA via Dana Bell*

A PBY "Black Cat" is flying a mission over a vast expanse of ocean on May 15, 1944. The Catalina had one of the most readily recognizable silhouettes among aircraft of World War II, with its prominent cabane strut supporting the wing. *NARA via Dana Bell*

This PBY-5A, operated by the Fighter Factory, is still flying over sixty years after it was built. When retracted, the rear wheels of the PBY-5A protruded slightly from the fuselage. The two white antennas on the wing outboard of the engines are postwar modifications. The proximity of the tips of the propellers when the engines are running is apparent. *Rich Kolasa*

The Fighter Factory PBY-5A in a three-color paint scheme cruises over a hazy landscape. This example has numerous postwar, civilian modifications, including three horizontal strengtheners on the skin of the fuselage to the rear of the cockpit, additional side windows, and a rudder whose top has been converted to a counterbalance that extends over the top of the vertical stabilizer, to improve handling. *Rich Kolasa*

From this angle, the manner in which the turret slightly obstructed the forward view of the pilot and copilot is evident. The cylinder protruding up at the side of the turret is the detachable mooring post. *Rich Kolasa*

This PBY-5A, originally US Navy BuNo 48294, was civilianized after the end of World War II. Subsequently, it was partially restored to its World War II military appearance, but it still retains some nonmilitary features. The two windows forward of the blister are nonstandard, as is the counterbalance at the top of the rudder, overhanging the top of the vertical stabilizer. *Rich Kolasa*

	PBY/PBN Catalina Specifications						
Model	**Gross weight**	**Max. speed @ altitude**	**Service ceiling**	**Patrol range**	**Number built**	**First delivery**	**Serial numbers**
XPBY-1	20,226 lbs.	184 mph @ 8,000 ft.	24,000	2,070	1	May 1936	9459
PBY-1	22,336 lbs.	175 mph @ 8,000 ft.	20,900	2,115	60	Sep. 1936	0102–0161
PBY-2	22,490 lbs.	178 mph @ 8,000 ft.	21,100	2,131	50	May 1937	0454–0503
PBY-3	22,713 lbs.	191 mph @ 12,000 ft.	24,400	2,175	66	Nov. 1937	0842–0907
PBY-4	24,813 lbs.	198 mph @ 12,000 ft.	24,100	2,070	32	May 1938	1213–1244
XPBY-5A	–	–	–	–	1	Nov. 1939	1245
PBY-5	31,813 lbs.	195 mph @ 7,000 ft.	17,700	2,860	684	Sep. 1940	2289–2455, 04425–04514, 08124–08549, 63992
PBY-5A	33,975 lbs.	180 mph @ 7,000 ft.	14,700	2,545	802	Oct. 1941	2456–2488, 02948–02977, 04399–04420, 05972–05045, 7243–7302, 08030–08123, 33960–34059, 46450–46638, 48252–48451
PBY-6A	34,550 lbs.	178 mph @ 7,000 ft.	16,200	2,535	175	May 1945	46639–46698, 46724, 63993–64106
PBN-1	36,553 lbs.	186 mph @ 6,700 ft.	15,100	2,590	155	Feb. 1943	02791–02946

The clear panels on the top front of the canopy of the PBY-5A could be slid backward on tracks mounted on either side of the Plexiglas panels to the rear. The three fuselage stiffeners to the rear of the fuselage are evidently postwar modifications, and the small window below the top pair of stiffeners is in a nonstandard configuration, insofar as the long side is vertical. Protruding from the center of the wing are fuel tank vents. *Rich Kolasa*

In the collections of the National Museum of Naval Aviation, Pensacola, Florida, is this display PBY-5A, US Navy registry number 46602. The vertical tail and rudder are as originally configured, as are the windows on the side of the fuselage. The fairings have been removed from the wing struts, exposing the wing/strut attachment points. *Author*

The PBY-5A's nosewheel, a closed-spoke design, was mounted on a split-type strut. In service in World War II, 30-inch tires with smooth treads were specified; this one is grooved. *Author*

The position of the forward port landing-gear door when opened is illustrated. The small vent to the rear of the door is one of two outlets for any water that might get trapped in the landing-gear bay when the doors were closed. *Author*

Because of the lack of clearance caused by the short landing gear, the two nose landing-gear doors were articulated to open to the sides and slightly upward. *Author*

As viewed on the starboard side of a PBY-5A nose landing gear, the axle is secured in a clamping-type mount, with a horizontal bolt at the rear of the mount and a vertical bolt at the front. *Author*

The top panels of the canopy are partially opened in this view from the wing of a PBY-5A. To the right, the port exhaust of the starboard engine is in view. *Rich Kolasa*

Small vents are set on the sides of the oil cooler housing. The cowl flaps were operated by the mechanic and were fully opened for engine starting, taxiing, takeoff, and landing. During steep climbs, the flaps were opened halfway. *Author*

The cowl flaps are open on this museum PBY-5A. To the rear of the nacelle is a circular inspection plate. Crossing diagonally through the view is the forward port wing strut. *Author*

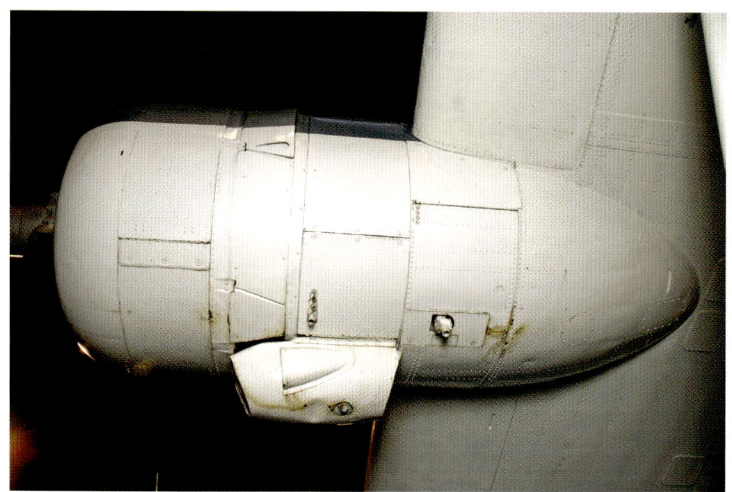

Starting with the PBY-5, the oil cooler was moved from the leading edge of the wing to below the engine nacelle. As shown on the port nacelle of a PBY-5A, the oil cooler intake was located to the starboard of the centerline; this was the case with both of the nacelles. An oil drain valve can be seen protruding through the plate aft of the oil cooler. *Author*

The Hamilton Standard Hydromatic propellers are revving up on a PBY-5A. The propellers were full-feathering and made from forged aluminum alloy. There is a horizontal splitter inside the mouth of the oil cooler intake. To the rear of the upper flap is a small air intake vent. *Rich Kolasa*

On both sides of the mechanic's station in the center wing pylon are small windows that enabled him to observe the engine nacelles and propellers. Below the window is a small air scoop. The top of the port main wheel well appears toward the bottom of the photo. *Author*

A fairing was fitted over each of the attachment points of the wing struts. The fairings at the bottoms of the two forward struts had cutouts at the bottom for the sockets that held the tops of the struts of the beaching gear. Even though PBY-5As had built-in landing gear, they retained this feature, since the beaching gear was often installed when servicing the landing gear. *Author*

The cylinder to the left of this photo, looking up toward the top of the port wheel well, is the main strut of the landing gear. The vertical groove in the wheel well housed the strut when the gear was retracted. The small, oval window allowed crewmen within the lower part of the mechanic's compartment to observe the landing gear. *Author*

The tires of the main landing gear were specified to be 47-inch Goodrich with smooth tread; this one is a 47-inch Goodyear with a diamond tread pattern. Stamped near the center of the open-spoked wheel are tire data and the wheel's part number and serial number. *Author*

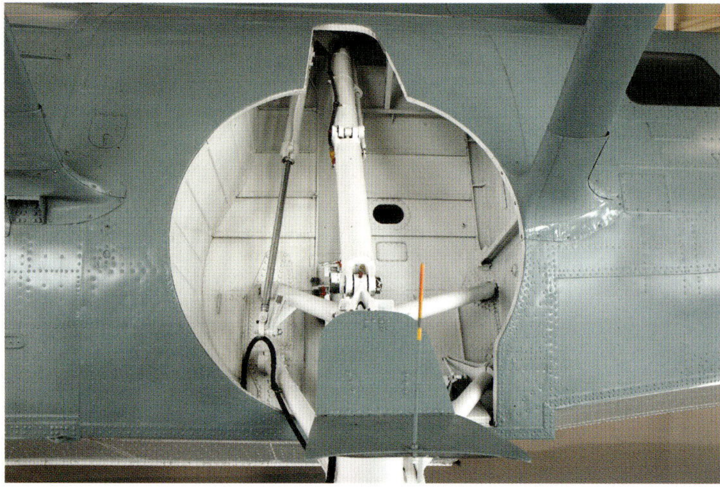

The folding door in the foreground sealed off the wheel well above the top of the wheel when the landing gear was retracted, thus reducing drag. On the forward side (to the left in this photo) of the main landing-gear strut is a hydraulically powered retraction strut, which is attached to the upper V-strut. The fairing of the rear wing strut is cut off to accommodate the wheel well. *Author*

Attached to the oleo strut (next to the wheel) are two V-struts, which, when extended, act to hold the oleo strut and wheel out from the fuselage as well as brace them. Hydraulic brake lines are routed along the forward edge of the lower V-strut. Emerging from the top of the wheel well is the main strut. *Author*

The front scissor of the port oleo strut is at the bottom of the strut. In wartime service, the brake lines were more compactly arranged at the bottom. Along the chine to the left of the photo are the two lower mounting brackets for the beaching gear. *Author*

The two port wing struts extend from the fuselage, with the landing gear between them. The front of the socket that accommodates the top of the beaching gear is visible. *Author*

Each of the PBY-5A's main landing gears has scissors on the front and rear of each oleo strut. The actuating link for the small, hinged door at the top of the oleo strut is above the scissors. *Author*

This PBY-5A is fitted with the black, unpainted brake lines that would have been seen on operational Catalinas during World War II. These lines are properly fitted, with just enough slack at the bottom. *Author*

Details of the port main landing gear, seen here from the rear, include the actuating link for the small door attached to the top of the oleo strut. The nose gear is visible toward the right. *Author*

The right wheel well of this example is painted matte white. Often, the wheel wells of PBY-5s were painted the same color as the adjacent fuselage. The actuating link that unfolds the wheel-well door when the landing gear is retracted is alongside the oleo strut. *Author*

To the lower rear of the main wheel when retracted is a small, white, nearly triangular door. When the landing gear is lowered, this door folds down inward, allowing clearance for the rear of the lower V-strut. *Rich Kolasa*

The U shape of the float strut is apparent adjacent to the float in this view of the underside of the port wing of a PBY-5A. Next to the float on the leading edge of the wing is the port navigation light, with a red lens and set in a housing that shielded the pilot from glare. *Author*

Tie-down eyes are mounted to the front and rear of the floats, to secure the aircraft when parked during windy conditions. The ailerons and the aft part of the wings were fabric over a metal frame. *Author*

Some of the blue paint on the top of the float (as it is oriented when lowered) shows from below when the float is retracted. The rear tie-down eye on the float is aligned parallel with the rear edge of the float. The wingspan of the PBY-5A was 104 feet when measured with the floats in the retracted position. During an electrical retraction-mechanism failure, the floats could be operated by means of a hand crank in the engineer's compartment. *Author*

Float Layout

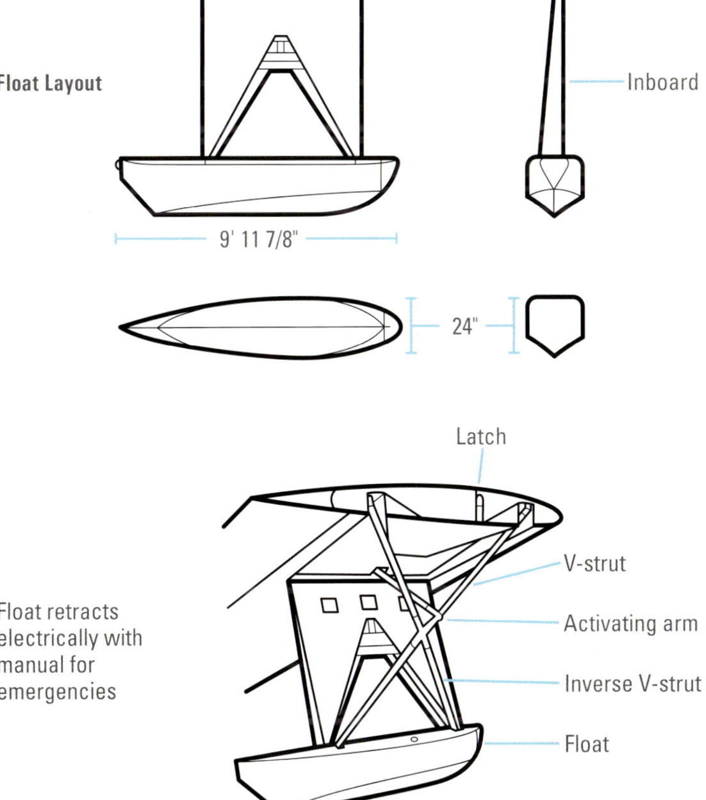

Float retracts electrically with manual for emergencies

The floats have been lowered on this PBY-5A in flight. Each float is mounted on a main strut that, when retracted, becomes an integral part of the lower wing surface. Outboard of the main struts are braces and actuating struts. *Rich Kolasa*

Each elevator of the Catalina was fitted with a trim tab toward the inboard side. The rudder of this PBY-5A has a modified balance at the top. *Author*

This PBY-5A has the standard rudder configuration, featuring a straight, vertical leading edge at the top of the rudder. Above the trim vane of the rudder is the taillight. *Author*

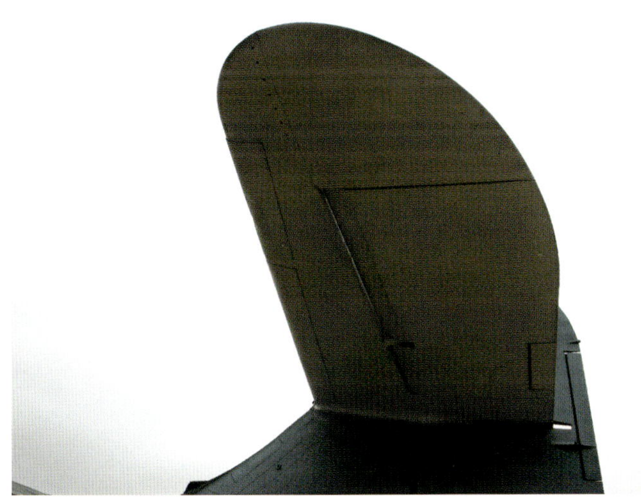

The center rear of the stabilizer passes through a cutout in the rudder. Below the cutout is the trim-tab control cable and horn. The elevator, like all the PBY control surfaces, is of dope and fabric-covered construction. The elevator had a range of movement from 29.75 degrees up to 19 degrees down. *Author*

The middle and rear portion of the blisters on each side of the PBY-5, -5A, and -6A formed a revolving door mounted on concentric pivots. When the door was rotated upward to the open position, the section of the blister toward the front of the aircraft acted as a windscreen. *Author*

The "eyeball" turret was introduced late in the manufacturing run of the PBY-5A and was retrofitted to some earlier models as well. The sides of the turret were similar to those of early PBYs, except a semispherical Plexiglas "eye" in a socket was installed at the front of the turret. Two .30-caliber machine guns protruded through this eye. Behind the eye and socket, at the front of the top of the turret, was an arched piece of Plexiglas, to allow the gunner upward visibility. *Author*

The eyeball turret protruded higher than the original type of turret and slightly obstructed the pilots' forward view. Behind the arched Plexiglas turret roof panel was a metal cover with a blister, to give the gunner headroom. Below and slightly aft of the turret is the anchor compartment. *Author*

The metal panel on the rear half of the turret roof was removable, allowing the crewmen to use the opening as a hatch for accessing the bow of the aircraft. *Author*

A metal rim was attached with Phillips-head screws around the opening of the fuselage adjacent to the turret, as a strengthener and to reduce draft. This Plexiglas, crystal clear when new, now shows the effects of years of exposure. *Author*

CHAPTER 3

Other Catalina Variants

Just as the PBY-5A was by far the most abundant Catalina, and the US Navy was the predominate user of the Catalina, there were other users of the aircraft, and further, lesser-known developments of the versatile seaplane.

The US Army also was a user of the Catalina, employing the aircraft chiefly in the air-sea rescue during World War II and well beyond. Most of the Army aircraft were PBY-5A, to which the Army assigned their own designation OA-10. In addition to the 105 OA-10s rostered by the Army Air Force, the service also had 230 OA-10A, which was that service's designation for the Canadian Vickers-built PBV-1A, while the 150 that entered RCAF service were known as the Canso A.

The USAAF also acquired seventy-five PBY-6A, which were designated OA-10B-CN in Army service.

The PBY-6A was the final model in the PBY line, produced in 1945 at the Consolidated Aircraft plant in New Orleans, Louisiana. Of 175 built, beyond the US Army Air Forces seventy-five, fifty-two were delivered to the US Navy, and forty-eight were shipped to the Soviets.

The PBY-6A differed from its predecessor in that it was equipped with radar, and more noticeably, featured the taller tail and rudder of the PBN-1 Nomad.

The PBN-1 had been developed and produced by the Naval Aircraft Factory. In addition to the taller tail, the PBN-1 differed from the PBY-5A in that it was almost 5 feet longer, had a redesigned bow and floats. Of the 156 PBN-1s built 1943-1945, the Navy used only seventeen of them, with the remainder going to the Soviet Union.

The Soviet Nomads joined the Russian-produced PBY-5 Catalina, the GST (*Gidrosamolet transportnii*, or seaplane transport), which were built under license from Consolidated in a plant in Taganrog, on the Sea of Azov beginning in 1938. Production of the aircraft was interrupted when the Germans captured the plant in October 1941, by which time only twenty-seven GSTs had been completed.

In addition to the Canadian Vickers PBV-1A, Boeing of Canada also produced Catalinas, or Cansos. Boeing Canada produced 240 PBY-5 flying boat Cansos. The six that entered US Navy service these aircraft were designated PB2B-1. Of the remaining 234 aircraft, seven were supplied to the RAAF (PB2B-1, serials A24-200 to A24-206), thirty-four to the RNZAF (NZ4023 to NZ4056), with the remainder of the production going to the RAF where they were designated the Catalina Mk IVB.

The PB2B-2 replaced the -1 on the Boeing Canada production line in September 1944. The PB2B-2 was not amphibious, instead utilizing beaching gear as had early models. It featured the tall tail of the PBN-1 Nomad and the eyeball gun turret characteristic of the PBY-6A, and like the -6A, was equipped with radar. Production of the PB2B-2 was discontinued in March 1945, after sixty-seven examples had been completed. Forty-seven of these went to the RAAF (PB2B-2, serials A24-300 to A24-309 and A24-350 to A24-386). The remaining twenty went to US forces, both Navy and Army.

While the US Navy was the prime user of the PBY Catalina, the US Army Air Forces acquired PBY-5As and PBY-6As to use for search-and-rescue aircraft in the vast expanses of the Pacific. Operating in emergency-rescue squadrons, these flying boats, given the USAAF designation OA-10s, located and rescued many downed Army Air Forces aircrewmen. Ultimately, the US Army Air Forces received 410 OA-10s of various models. Shown here is OA-10A-VI USAAF, serial number 44-33876, of the 2nd Emergency Rescue Squadron "Snafu Snatchers," flying a patrol mission near the Dutch East Indies in 1944. It was one of 230 OA-10A-VIs produced by Canadian Vickers to PBY-5A standards and supplied to the US Army Air Forces. *National Museum of the United States Air Force*

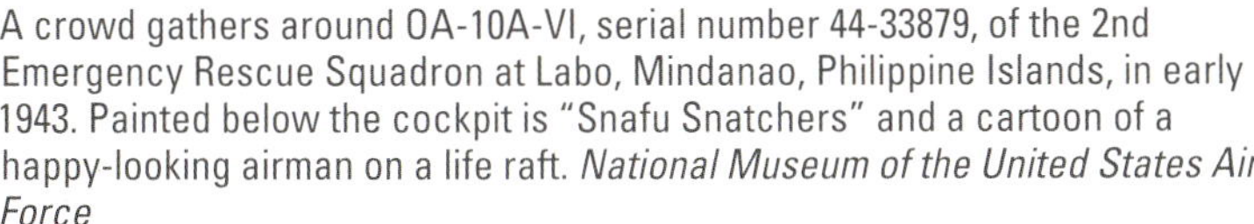

A crowd gathers around OA-10A-VI, serial number 44-33879, of the 2nd Emergency Rescue Squadron at Labo, Mindanao, Philippine Islands, in early 1943. Painted below the cockpit is "Snafu Snatchers" and a cartoon of a happy-looking airman on a life raft. *National Museum of the United States Air Force*

OA-10A-VI, serial number 44-33879, of the 2nd Emergency Rescue Squadron at Labo, Mindanao, in early 1945, is viewed from the front. Instead of the RDF loop antenna at the top center of the wing, an RDF "football" antenna housing has been installed there. *National Museum of the United States Air Force*

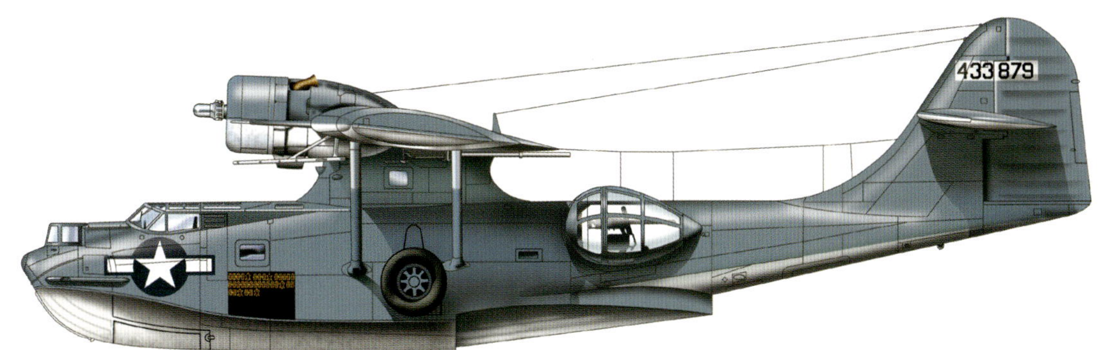

USAAF OA-10A, serial number 44-33879, of the 2nd Emergency Rescue Squadron "Snafu Snatchers," operated in the Southwest Pacific area. On the hull below the navigator's window was a black scoreboard listing over fifty rescues.

Natives paddle out to a USAAF Consolidated OA-10 anchored in a bay in the Philippines around early 1945. The flying boat had come to land a special reconnaissance party, and Filipinos reported the locations of Japanese naval mines to the crew of the OA-10. *National Archives*

The OA-10A-VI shown in the preceding photograph, serial number 44-33882, is viewed from the port side at Middleburg Island. Yagi radar arrays are apparent under the wings, and in the upper foreground, a Yagi radar antenna from another aircraft is in view. *National Museum of the United States Air Force*

An OA-10 of the 5th Emergency Rescue Group was photographed in New Guinea. The ubiquitous Yagi radar arrays are present. Previously named the 5276th Rescue Composite Group, this unit was redesignated the 5th Emergency Rescue Group in April 1945. *National Museum of the United States Air Force*

The crew of OA-10A-VI, serial number 44-33882, of Flight C, 2nd Emergency Rescue Squadron, pose in front of their Catalina at Middleburg Island, New Guinea, in 1944. The number "82" is on the bow, and auxiliary fuel tanks are mounted under the wing. *National Museum of the United States Air Force*

An OA-10 has the self-descriptive name "Air-Sea Rescue" written in attractive script on the side of the hull. Below that name is written in smaller script "Cheryl Ann." In addition to the Yagi radar arrays under the wings, a radome is mounted atop the canopy. *National Museum of the United States Air Force*

In late 1948, OA-10 44-33950 of the 10th Rescue Squadron prepares for takeoff on a practice mission from Lake Cheletna, Alaska. The aircraft was equipped with two jet-assisted takeoff (JATO) units on each side of the hull, below and aft of the blisters. *National Museum of the United States Air Force*

Many of the OA-10s featured all-white paint schemes. Black deicer boots are on the leading edges of the wing, horizontal stabilizers, and vertical fin. In addition to the Yagi receiver arrays under the wing, a broadside receiver array is on the hull, below the engine. *National Museum of the United States Air Force*

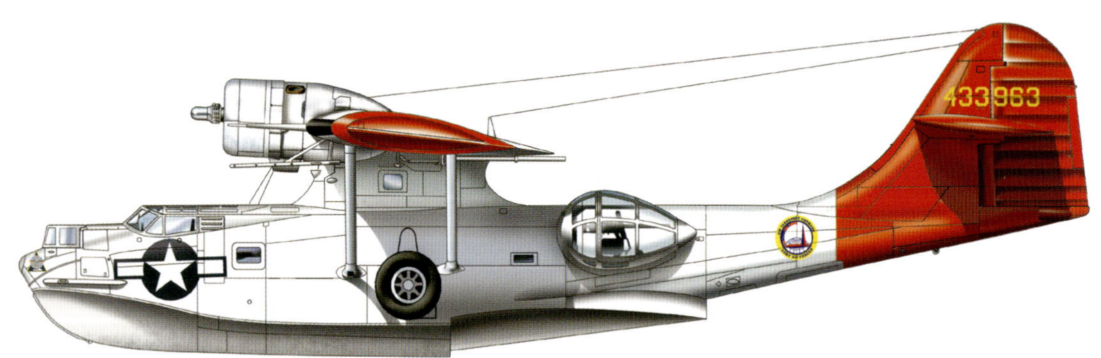

Army OA-10A Catalinas assigned to the Alaskan Division of the Air Transport Command in 1946 wore this colorful scheme of white and Insignia Red.

US Air Force OA-10A-VI, serial number 44-33939, assigned to the 4th Rescue Squadron at Hamilton Air Force Base, California, sported a very colorful postwar paint scheme, with yellow high-visibility areas and red sections, in addition to the base colors. *National Museum of the United States Air Force*

OA-10A-VI, serial number 44-33939, is viewed from the aft port quarter while serving with the 4th Rescue Squadron at Hamilton Air Force Base. On the yellow panel below the cockpit canopy is "ARS4R9" in black letters. Worthy of notice is the manner in which the blue-gray paint wrapped around the bend, or chine, of the hull, below and aft of the waist blisters, and also was applied to the vertical part of the step of the hull, underneath the waist blisters. Yagi radar arrays are below the wing, and a radome is above the cockpit canopy. During World War II, while stationed at Foggia, Italy, this aircraft had an overall white paint scheme. *National Museum of the United States Air Force*

OA-10A-VI, serial number 44-33999, boasts a high-visibility scheme for a postwar USAF rescue plane. On the yellow placard below and adjacent to the cockpit is "OB-999." The number "999" is in large yellow numerals with black borders on the bottom of the hull. *National Museum of the United States Air Force*

A US Air Force air-sea rescue OA-10A exhibits a postwar paint scheme and markings, including a panel with "OB-939" alongside the cockpit. *Stan Piet collection*

On display at the National Museum of the US Air Force is Consolidated PBY-5A, BuNo 46595 and construction number 1959. It was located in Brazil in the early 1980s and delivered to the National Museum of the US Air Force in 1984. By the late 1980s, the plane had been restored and painted to replicate Canadian Vickers OA-10A Catalina, serial number 44-33879, which served with the US Army Air Forces' 2nd Emergency Rescue Squadron "Snafu Snatchers" in the southwestern Pacific in World War II. The squadron's "Snafu Snatchers" nickname and a depiction of a downed airman on a life raft were painted on the right side of the squadron's Catalinas. *National Museum of the United States Air Force*

The engine nacelles, propellers, center wing support pylon, and cockpit canopy are viewed from the right side. On the bottoms of the nacelles are the oil-cooler housings, with air scoops on the sides. Midway up on the leading edge of the pylon is a step. *National Museum of the United States Air Force*

The PBY-5A restored to represent OA-10A Catalina serial number 44-33879 is parked on a tarmac at the National Museum of the US Air Force, at Wright-Patterson Air Force Base, outside Dayton, Ohio. It is painted in a Blue Gray over Light Gray camouflage. *National Museum of the United States Air Force*

While the one hundred Catalina I aircraft had been purchased directly by the RAF, in 1942 Consolidated produced 225 flying boats based on the PBY-5 for delivery to the British via Lend-Lease; these were designated the PBY-5B by the US Navy and Catalina IB by the British. This Catalina II bears the serial number FP111 at the base of the vertical fin. This was the twelfth of 225 Catalina IIs delivered to the British. Yagi radar antennas are below the wings and along the forward fuselage. *National Archives*

Serial numbers FP100 to FP324 were assigned to the RAF aircraft Catalina I. Ultimately, sixty of the RAF-contract aircraft were delivered to the US Navy, with 165 going to the RAF. *National Archives*

Intended for delivery to the RAF with serial number FP216, this PBY-5B was damaged in a water-looping accident in East Bay, Pensacola, Florida, on May 28, 1944, and deemed unfit for further flight. It was decided that the hull and a portion of starboard wing would be retained as a training aid, as shown here. This aircraft survives today as a cutaway exhibit in the National Museum of Naval Aviation. *San Diego Air and Space Museum*

Originally intended for delivery to the British, this PBY-5B, assigned British serial number FP216, was badly damaged in an accident while being used as a trainer at Pensacola, Florida, in May 1944. Rather than write off the airframe, the Navy built it, minus its outer wings and the left engine, into a wall of the Survival Training Unit Building at Naval Air Station Pensacola. Various skin panels were removed, resulting in a cutaway Catalina. When the building was slated for demolition in the mid-1990s, the PBY Catalina International Association raised funds to preserve the PBY-5 at the National Museum of Naval Aviation, in Pensacola. *Robert Bohlmann*

The anchor compartment below and to the rear of the turret on the port side of the cutaway PBY-5B is shown open, with the compartment door raised at the top of the photo. The brass chock with the diagonal slot on the side of the chine rail acted to secure the anchor cable when the anchor was lowered. The line running from the anchor compartment to the bow is the pendant, the lower end of which was permanently fastened to a fitting on the keel. The hole in the fuselage skin to the upper rear of the anchor compartment originally held a pullout step to assist crewmen in moving between the deck in front of the cockpit and the chine rail. *Robert Bohlmann*

An opening in the port side of the cutaway PBY-5B allows a view of a Norden bombsight in its position in the nose. The top of the stabilizer unit of the bombsight is toward the bottom, with the bombsight head on top of it. The box on the side of the stabilizer unit with the data plate and two aluminum-colored covers is the directional panel, which was connected to the autopilot. *Author*

The shutters over the bombardier's window, shown in the lowered position, were intended to protect the window from the wear and tear the bow of the aircraft endured during takeoffs and landings. *Author*

Just to the side of the bombsight window is a circular hand hole with cover. The cover, shown here, is removable to the inside of the aircraft. This permitted the bombardier to reach out and wipe the bombsight window clean while the PBY was in flight. *Author*

The cutaway PBY display at the National Museum of Naval Aviation, Pensacola, Florida, comprises the fuselage of a PBY-5B (or Catalina IB) originally earmarked for the Royal Air Force, registration number FP216. The aircraft was damaged in an accident, and the wing was removed and sections were cut from the port side of the fuselage to turn it into a cutaway display for training purposes. An opening in the front of the turret accommodates the barrel of a .30-caliber machine gun, on which is mounted a one-hundred-round ammunition box; the smaller box on the other side of the gun is the spent-link box. *Author*

This aircraft has an early-type, flat-top nose turret with curved sections of glass set into a circular frame. At the rear of the top of the turret is a detachable, D-shaped cover with a clear panel inset in it. Removing the cover allowed crewmen to climb out on the front deck and the chine rails on either side of the nose to perform various operations, including setting the mooring lines and dropping or raising the anchor. On the port side of the forward part of the roof is a removable holder for a spotlight. *Author*

Racks for .30-caliber ammunition boxes are inside the bombardier/gunner's compartment, on the left. The purpose of the curtain with zippered door panel to the right at the rear of the compartment was to cut down drafts from the compartment into the cockpit. Such drafts could be fierce when the turret cover was removed. *Author*

The large box on top of the yoke housed the visual signal system, by which the pilot and mechanic could communicate concerning various mechanical functions without using the intercom. The knob with the quadrant scale below it, on the bottom of the instrument panel to the right of the pilot's control wheel, is the aileron trim tab control. *Author*

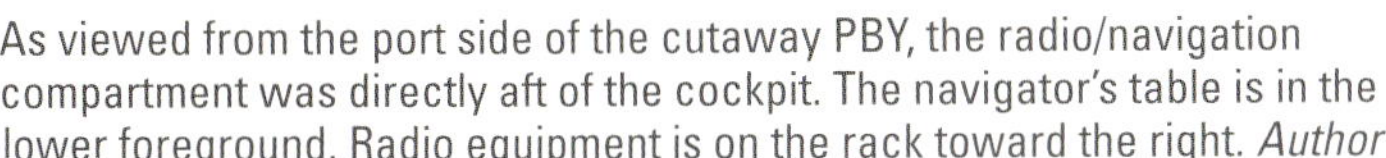

As viewed from the port side of the cutaway PBY, the radio/navigation compartment was directly aft of the cockpit. The navigator's table is in the lower foreground. Radio equipment is on the rack toward the right. *Author*

Below the GO-9 transmitter is its mounting rack. On the underside of the radio operator's table was a drawer and a cabinet. *Author*

Visible on the pilot's seat are the adjusting lever, shoulder harness, and armrests. On the top of the canopy are the throttles and propeller and mixer controls. A pouch for a pelorus, a navigational instrument that could be mounted on the upper corners of the windshield, is on the rear bulkhead of the cockpit. *Author*

On the rack above the radioman's table are two RU-19 radio receivers, between which is an LM-10 frequency meter. The trailing antenna reel is to the far left. A telegraph key was usually mounted toward the aft outboard corner of the radioman's table (out of view to the right). *Author*

A mannequin represents the mechanic sitting in his bucket seat; his left foot is on a footrest over the door leading to the radio/navigation compartment. In front of the mannequin is the mechanic's instrument panel. The handles with red knobs at the top of the panel are the mixture controls for the engines. *Author*

The mechanic's instrument panel was painted black and was shaped with a taper toward the top to fit inside the cabane strut. The panel included many of the gauges that were present on the pilot's instrument panel, and above the gauges are the switches and indicators of the visual signal system. Visible to the right of the mixture controls at the top of the panel is the forward sight gauge for the right engine's fuel system; the placard at the top right of the photo gave instructions for reading the gauges. *Author*

Extending below the APU are rubber suction lines from the bilge to the bilge pump. Dangling at the top left is the foot of a mannequin in the mechanic's seat, while a mannequin representing the radio operator is visible beyond the door to the left. The living compartment is to the right. *Author*

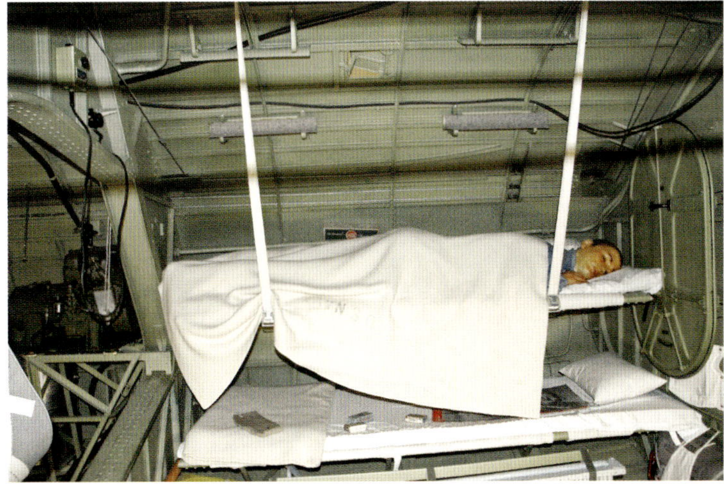

A mannequin here represents a crewman sleeping in the upper starboard bunk in the living compartment. To the left is bulkhead 5, separating the living quarters from the mechanic's compartment. The auxiliary power unit (APU) is to the upper left, in the position it occupied in the PBY-5, at the starboard rear corner of the mechanic's compartment. In the PBY-5A, the APU was moved to the forward port side of the mechanic's compartment. *Author*

There was an upper bunk on the starboard side only; the port side had a single bunk. A canvas cover is snapped over the small window above the upper bunk. A pouch for storing a life jacket is below the door, and an inflatable life jacket and a parachute harness are lying on the lower bunk. *Author*

As viewed from the port side of the cutaway PBY, the tunnel compartment aft of the machine gunners' compartment contains several types of signal flares as well as two flare ejector tubes (*left of center*). *Author*

Clipped on the bulkhead at the front of the tunnel compartment are buoyant signal flares, otherwise known as Mk. IV aircraft float lights. Consisting of a wooden body filled with explosives, with a metal tail to stabilize them when dropped, the float lights served many purposes, including marking the positions of downed airmen and plotting the course of enemy submarines. The port flare ejector tube is to the right. *Author*

The port side of the tunnel, the compartment aft of the waist gunners' compartment, is viewed from the rear. The tunnel machine gun mount is in its stored position inboard of the flares stored on the side of the compartment. One of two flare ejector tubes is visible in the right background. The white labels on the black flares contain directions for use. *Author*

The PB2B-2, a version of the Catalina produced by Boeing of Canada, consisted of a late PBY-5A airframe to which was mated a PBN-1 Nomad empennage. The British and Australians operated them as the Catalina VI and the Americans as the PB2B-2. *National Museum of Naval Aviation*

The PBN-1 Nomad was the US Navy's own take on the PBY Catalina. The Naval Aircraft Factory in Philadelphia, Pennsylvania, developed and manufactured the Nomad, taking the basic Consolidated PBY-5 airframe and redesigning certain elements, including the bow, the bow turret, the floats, and the empennage. The aft part of the fuselage was extended by 56 inches, the fuel tanks were enlarged, and a new bombardier's window was included. Of the 156 PBN-1 Nomads produced from February 1943 to March 1945, the US Navy received seventeen and the Soviets received the balance. *National Archives*

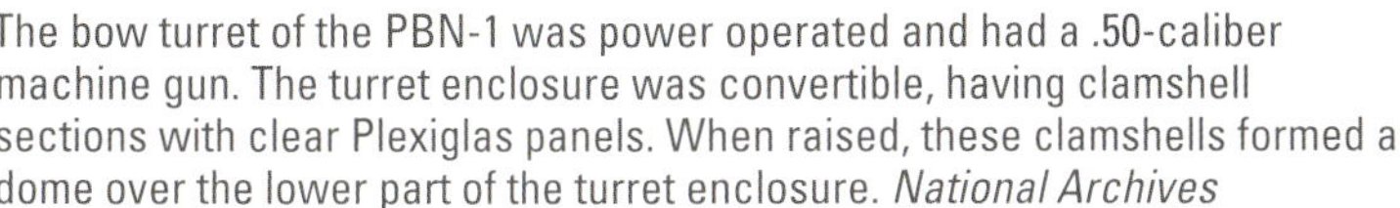

The bow turret of the PBN-1 was power operated and had a .50-caliber machine gun. The turret enclosure was convertible, having clamshell sections with clear Plexiglas panels. When raised, these clamshells formed a dome over the lower part of the turret enclosure. *National Archives*

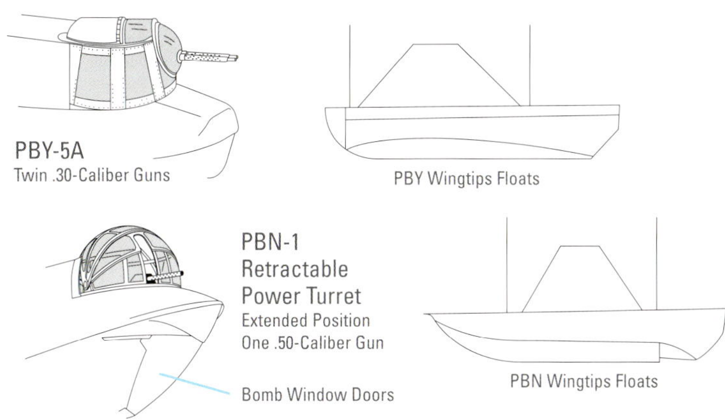

The relative shapes of the eyeball turret of late PBY-5As and the bow turret of the PBN-1 Nomad are illustrated. In the bow of the PBN-1 were doors that covered the bombardier's window. The different designs of the floats of the PBY-5A and PBN-1 are also shown.

With the PBN-1 Nomad's turret clamshell sections lowered and the flat cover removed from the turret enclosure, the receiver of the .50-caliber machine gun, the ammunition box holder, and other elements inside the turret are visible. *National Archives*

When the bow turret of the PBN-1 was not in use, the clamshell sections of the turret enclosure were lowered and a flat cover was placed over the opening at the top of the turret enclosure, both to reduce drag and to give the pilot and copilot better visibility. *National Archives*

The PBY-6A shared the late PBY-5A's eyeball turret, tricycle landing gear, and Pratt & Whitney R-1830-92 engines but added a radome over the cockpit canopy and grafted on the empennage of the PBN-1 Nomad. This USN PBY-6A, BuNo 64063, was part of a 114-plane production block completed between May and September 1945. *National Museum of Naval Aviation*

This PBY-6A was assigned to the Navy Reserve and as such had orange bands around the aft part of the hull. The paint scheme was Glossy Sea Blue overall; radomes were white. *National Museum of Naval Aviation*

PBY-6A, BuNo 46662, photographed on August 28, 1955, was assigned to Corry Field, Pensacola, Florida. The aircraft was painted overall Glossy Sea Blue with yellow hull band and wing panels and splotchy, discolored fabric on the rear half of the wing. *National Museum of Naval Aviation*

Seen on November 11, 1953, is US Navy PBY-6A, BuNo 64071, based at NAS Barbers Point, Oahu. This PBY later flew under various civilian owners before it crashed and sank in the Tagus River, Portugal, on June 28, 1979. *National Museum of Naval Aviation*

US Air Force OA-10B, serial number 45-57834, was assigned to the 1st Rescue Squadron. The aircraft exhibits an overall white paint scheme with a yellow, black-bordered band near the tail. On the panel adjacent to the cockpit is "AR 1RS." *National Museum of the United States Air Force*

The black panel on the side of the forward fuselage of a PBY-5A restored to represent an OA-10A is a scoreboard of rescues performed by the crew of the Catalina. The 2nd Emergency Rescue Squadron was credited with rescuing over seven hundred Allied airmen during World War II. PBY flying boats performed stellar service in World War II and after. It was PBYs that discovered the German battleship *Bismarck* as it broke out into the North Atlantic, and PBYs that spotted the Japanese fleet as it approached the Midway Islands in June 1942. PBYs helped hold the line in the Aleutian Islands, patrolled vast expanses of ocean, conducted raids, ferried supplies to outposts, and saved many a downed airman. Slow but durable and long legged, the PBY Catalina was indeed one of the outstanding aircraft of World War II. *National Museum of the United States Air Force*